CHRIST CONQUERS

Why Christ Rose on Sunday, the First Day of the Week

The Vital Relation to Armageddon, the Battle of That Great Day of God Almighty!

By Louis F. Were

CHRIST CONQUERS

OR

Why Christ Rose on Sunday, the First Day of the Week

By Louis F. Were

© 1999 by Laymen Ministries/
LMN Publishing International, Inc.

ISBN: 978-0-9961896-5-1

Published by:
LAYMEN MINISTRIES
414 Zapada Rd.
St. Maries, ID 83861
Orders: (800)245-1844   Office: (208)245-5388

Website/Bookstore: www.lmn.org

Truth transcends Personalities, Politics, and Parties.

"The only question which any wise man can ask himself, and which any honest man will ask himself, is whether a doctrine is true or false." —Huxley.

"O what a goodly outside falsehood hath." —Shakespeare.

"Generality is the cloak of fiction, while minuteness is the mantle of truth."

CONTENTS

KEY TO ABBREVIATIONS

1T, 2T, etc. . . . . . . *Testimonies,* Vol. 1, Vol. 2, etc.

AA . . . . *The Acts of the Apostles*

1BC, 2BC, etc. . . . *SDA Bible Commentary,* Vol. 1, Vol. 2, etc.

COL . . . .*Christ's Object Lessons*

DA . . . . *The Desire of Ages*

EW . . . . *Early Writings*

GC . . . . *The Great Controversy*

GW . . . . *Gospel Workers*

MH . . . . *Ministry of Healing*

PK . . . . *Prophets and Kings*

PP . . . . *Patriarchs and Prophets*

RH . . . . *Review and Herald*

SP . . . .*The Spirit of Prophecy*

TM . . . . *Testimonies to Ministers*

Other referenced publications may no longer be in print.

*Note: Emphasis to extracts employed has been added to draw attention to certain salient features.

The references in this edition have been carefully checked, and as a result, may differ slightly in some cases from the original text. Every effort has been made to ensure that all references are accurate.

Introduction

It may surprise some to learn that there is a definite connection between the resurrection of our matchless Lord on Sunday, the first day of the week, and "Armageddon," "the battle of the great day of God Almighty." However, such, positively, is the teaching of the prophecies of the Scripture. Nothing in all the last-day predictions is more clearly taught than that "the final conflict" is to be fought between two Kingdoms—God's and Satan's. On the one hand, Satan's Babylonian forces march under the sign of "the mark of the beast," while, on the other side, the armies of Jesus, the deathless Lord, march under the banner of "the sign, or the seal, of the living God." This is not a matter of speculation, or of opinion—it is the clear light of God's revelation; a fact which is established upon irrefutable evidence obtained from the Bible and the Spirit of Prophecy.

When reading the Bible, two persons must always be considered—Christ, and His adversary Satan. Every chapter and verse must be read in the light of the conflict which rages between these two kings—representing two opposing kingdoms. No sooner had the Son of God (working in conjunction with His Father) created this world, than Lucifer, the fallen angel, turned the cunning of his mighty intellect to the contemptible task of ruining what our infinite Lord has created.

"Thy thoughts are very deep," said the Psalmist, of the Lord's wisdom and knowledge. Lucifer also, in his cunning designs, and in the execution of his plots, has revealed that originally he was created with tremendous potentialities along constructive lines. He has turned his gigantic intellect into channels of destruction. No human mind, under ordinary circumstances, could have been capable of matching strength of mind with his. Now that man has sinned, he cannot, of his own judgment, always know when he is doing, or not doing, the will of the wily foe. In His blessed Word, God has repeatedly counseled us not to walk according to the dictates of our own hearts or minds. We are urged to heed very carefully the instructions and the injunctions of Holy Writ, as the only way of avoiding being deceived by Satanic sophistries. (See Jer. 17:5-7; 10:23; Prov. 3:5-7; etc.)

When Satan fails in one deception he tries another. "There is nothing that the great deceiver fears so much as that we shall become acquainted with his devices . . . It is an evidence of his success that theories giving the lie to the plainest testimony of the Scriptures are so generally received in the religious world." GC 516, 517.

This outline contains some helpful and valuable extracts dealing with the origin, and continuance, of Sunday and other festivals which have come down to us from the ancient world of sun-worshippers. These facts help us to more readily understand the significance of the final conflict between truth and error, which involves Christ, spiritual Israel and the Sabbath, on the one side; and Satan, the forces of Babylon and Sun-day worship, on the other side.

To properly understand the end of the controversy between Christ and Satan it is necessary to study it from its commencement, and to follow its progress down through the centuries. The principles involved in the controversy are the same to-day as in the incipient stages. Satan, however, has learned much by his experience along the corridors of human history, and he will exploit to the full all that his inventive mind has conceived since sin began. But, no matter how much he may change the appearance of his plans, they are the same as ever. By acquainting ourselves with the past we learn much about the future. History will repeat itself—with this exception: events of the past which are recorded in the Scriptures were limited to some place, whereas, in the final conflict the whole world will be involved. That is why the Revelator takes all the events which occurred locally in connection with ancient, national Israel, and applies them in a world-wide setting. The Apocalypse is full of this principle, and from this angle alone (and there are many other reasons which establish the same fact) "Armageddon" cannot possibly refer to a Palestinian conflict. These features are considered in my "What Is 'Armageddon'?" I have been greatly encouraged as I have received letters of appreciation from different countries of the world. In my next publication: "Armageddon—Before and After the Millennium," additional evidence is presented to prove conclusively that the Palestinian "Armageddon" is not a part of the Third Angel's Message, but, instead, in principle, is actually opposed to it.

Adelaide, Australia
January 4th, 1944   LOUIS F. WERE

CHAPTER 1

Lucifer—the Day Star—Introduces Sin

G od moves in a mysterious way His wonders to perform." Infinite wisdom and love prompt all of God's actions—His view comprehends eternity.

The plan of salvation, centered in Christ, was devised to make the universe happy and contented through ceaseless cycles under Jehovah's benign scepter. Each event in the earthly experiences of the great Redeemer was designed to establish the everlasting foundations of righteousness, by meeting and conquering evil. On the other hand, the evil one was working to over-throw righteousness. From the time Satan introduced sin into the world he opposed God's redemptive plan—selecting the most essential features for the exercise of his most subtle and yet determined opposition.

In the courts of heaven, Lucifer was the highest intelligence next to the Deity, favoured as a covering cherub to their glorious Majesties, and was the beloved leader of the choir of heaven. Ezek. 28:13-17. His heavenly name was Lucifer, which means "Day Star." Isa. 14:12-14 margin. He was so brilliant that he shone as a sun. The righteous, who will occupy a similar place among the angels (Zech. 3:7), will then "shine forth as the sun in the kingdom of their Father." Matt. 13:43. Originally made perfect (Ezek. 28:15), yet endowed with the priceless heritage of freedom of choice (Rev. 22:17; Deut. 30:15-19), Lucifer chose the ways of selfishness. Selfishness in any form unbalances the judgment—engenders pride, vanity and conceit, and a stubborn self-will. Thus a vicious circle is formed which, without grace, by the very constitution of things, can only become worse with experience and the passage of time.

God, by His very nature, must have given Lucifer ample grace to retrace his steps—to acknowledge his errors and restore the will of God to its rightful place in his heart. When Lucifer first began to think in selfish terms his thoughts were easily read by the Infinite One. Ps. 139:1-12; Heb. 4:13. By His Omniscience, God could see the terrible future resulting from the selfish *thinking* of the covering cherub.

WHY GOD DID NOT DESTROY LUCIFER

Why did not God immediately destroy Lucifer, thus preventing the awful agonies, which, ever since, have cursed God's creation? Infinite Wisdom knew that, should He destroy Lucifer, the love and peace of his subjects would be gone forever, and the very situation He would endeavour to save would, in that very act, be brought into existence. Eternal happiness for the unnumbered worlds in God's illimitable universe must, and will, be established upon confidence in the love and wisdom of the Creator. Destroying Lucifer, without his *thoughts* being revealed in action, would forever destroy the possibility of heavenly harmony. And, once a free-moral creature violated heaven's law of love, and thus experimented in ways foreign to God, that experiment must be allowed to run its full course of evil. Sin must show itself to be the cause of misery, suffering, wretchedness—the spoiler of the lovely, the beautiful, the noble, the grand. With the full knowledge of its frightful consequences, free-moral creatures will, of their own choice, determinedly choose the perfect Will of God.

So Lucifer, in his exalted position, stately and glorious in person and revered by the angels, was not destroyed when he began his evil course. The holy angels in their innocence did not dream, could not dream, of the evil growing within Lucifer's heart, nor of the tragedies to follow. Only as the proud angel worked out his selfishness could finite intelligences know the evil within a beautiful form.

LUCIFER COMES TO THIS EARTH

When Lucifer—the light-bearer—came to earth, it was with the avowed purpose of continuing his selfishness under the guise of a benefactor to the human family, while exalting his will above God's will. His method in heaven was to appear to be the lightbearer, even though leading in rebellion against God. On earth he follows the same course. In Eden he deceived Eve to believe she would be better off by following his plan—her spirit would be freer. He insinuated that those who obeyed God were under bondage—a spiritual slavery. Those who disobeyed experienced the thrill of self-emancipation—the sweetness of doing one's own will. The joy of choosing one's own path was real liberty. And, under this strange infatuation, it seemed that God desired obedience to His will for selfish reasons! All this is in the original temptation recorded in Gen. 3:1-8. The light-bearer—the vaunted liberty bringer—thus brought darkness and bondage to our world. And what bondage—held as captives to the will of Satan (2 Peter 2:19; 2 Tim. 2:26)! Not under a loving will which desires good for all, but under a selfish will which desires everything for itself. Not under a will which brings joy, peace and happiness, a joyous liberty and real freedom, but under a will which desires no one's good but its own exaltation.

Accusing God of seeking the groveling subjection of His creatures, Satan soon began to manifest that as his own desire. God seeks the surrender of our will to His—but only "for our good always" (Deut. 6:24; 33:2-3), and that, too, with our intelligent appreciation of that fact (Rev. 11:17; 15:3; 19:1-6), as the outcome of the growth of our characters, which learn the value of God's holiness. Satan seeks to force the surrender of our will merely for the supremacy of his will.

SIN BEGINS TO BEAR FRUIT

Satan had not long conquered man's will—thus bringing this planet under his control—when sin began to show itself to be the hideous thing that it is. The first boy born into the Satan-controlled world followed that path of selfishness which seeks the *domination of others*. Cain demanded that Abel offer sacrifices as he willed. Satan's vaunted "freedom" for one's self was translated into murder. *All selfishness is potential murder.* Down through six thousand years of earthly history, individuals and nations have proved that the will unsurrendered to God means death to one's fellows. For, when two selfish wills seek the same thing, the struggle for supremacy causes bitterness and hatred—and death wherein opportunity affords.

Cain and Abel are the historic prototypes of the world's two classes—one, following the impulses of self-will, trampling ruthlessly the rights of others in order to be supreme; the other seeking to do God's will, and thus in love, remembering the rights and interests of their fellow-creatures. The former seek to destroy even those who desire only their good, simply because their will is not acknowledged as being first; while the latter would preserve the rights of even those who would kill them did opportunity come.

Cain in his selfish freedom was the slave of Satan; likewise all those who are unsurrendered to God. Lucifer—the light-bearer—brought spiritual darkness to this world, but Jesus, the true light-bearer, "the Light of the World," came in His humble splendour—the glory of a pure and undefiled character—to bring everlasting light to those who follow Him.

CHAPTER II

East—the Place of Sunrise

When God created the world and all of the things in it, He did not make the whole of Eden a garden. Only a portion of Eden was planted with a garden by the Creator. Concerning this garden the Divine Record says, "And the Lord God planted a garden Eastward in Eden; and there He put the man whom He had formed." Gen. 2:8.

The Inspired Penman makes clear what God did to man when He yielded to the great deceiver:—"Therefore the Lord sent him forth from the Garden of Eden,... so He drove out the man; and He placed *at the East* of the garden of Eden cherubims, and a flaming sword which turned every way to keep the way of the tree of life." Gen. 3:23, 24. Driven from the "garden eastward *in* Eden" our first parents and their children worshipped God *"at the east* of the garden of Eden." In worshipping God their backs would be to the east.

When self-willed Cain left home he turned his back upon the place where the Lord was worshipped, and journeyed towards the rising sun. "And Cain went *out from* the presence of the Lord, and dwelt in the land of Nod, on *the east* of Eden." Gen. 4:16. *Spiritually*, mankind has followed this easterly direction ever since.

From the early days of the human family the sun has been worshipped, and has been the predominating feature in false systems of religion.

The sun, rising in all its splendours after the darkness of the night, instead of being the *symbol* of "the Light of the world," became the *literal* object of worship by self-willed, and yet enslaved, man.

Cain, going "out from the presence of the Lord," and turning toward the rising sun, found (like the Prodigal Son) a sense of freedom in going away from his Father's presence. Imposed by God's holiness, there are wise prohibitions, loving restrictions, and necessary restraints in God's everlasting kingdom. Rebellious man seeks to do his own will without restraint. The system of sun-worship gave man the avenue of escape, and enabled him to render homage to a supernatural being in a way pleasing to self-will.

PARTIAL, OR COMPLETE OBEDIENCE?

Man loves to choose *which* of God's Commandments he will obey. This is why James wrote as he did in Chapter 2:10-12 of his book. He says: "Whosoever keepeth the whole law, and yet offends in *one point*, is guilty of *all*." He points out that a partial obedience to God's Commandments is insufficient to meet the requirements of holiness, because it is tantamount to obeying only that which pleases man's self-will. That is, man obeys where he pleases, and disobeys where he does not wish to obey. Deliberate partial obedience is idolatry—placing self-will before God's will. "Man shall not live by bread alone but by *every* word that proceedeth out of the mouth of God." Matt. 4:4. Many instances are recorded in Scripture where God refused the worship of those who rendered only partial obedience. "Christ is either Lord of all, or He is not Lord at all."

Sun-worship became that form of religion in which man was permitted to exercise his self-will by offering such worship as appealed to his selfishness, and rendering partial obedience, which gratified pride. If a man can choose which commands he will obey, his will is supreme, above even God's will, for in choosing which Commandments he will obey he makes the desideratum not God's authority, but his own.

The Bible gives us the record of the selfish choice of Lot as an example of all self-pleasing. Lot was reared and cared for by his uncle, but the time came when the size of their families and flocks required them to part company. Abraham magnanimously gave Lot first choice in the selection of the country. Lot greedily chose the best. "And Lot lifted up his eyes, and beheld all the plain of Jordan, that it was well watered everywhere… even as the garden of the Lord." Note the significant wording of the next verse. "Then Lot chose him all the plain of Jordan; and Lot *journeyed East*, and they separated themselves the one from the other…. Lot pitched his tent toward Sodom. But the men of Sodom *were wicked and sinners before the Lord exceedingly*." Gen. 13:5-15.

BABYLON

As the human family grew in numbers and spread over the earth Satan sought to establish a worldly empire further to the East—in Babylon.

"And it came to pass, as they *journeyed eastward* (margin) that they found a plain in the land of Shinar; and they dwelt there." Gen. 11:2. There they built the Tower of Babel in their rebellion against the Lord. The intervention of God brought them confusion. "Therefore is the name of it called Babel," margin, "confusion." Gen. 11:9. In the city of Babylon, which afterwards arose on this eastern plain, self-will was manifested in a system of religion which has exercised more influence upon mankind than most people imagine.

When God wished to oppose this system centered in man's selfishness (which is Satan's bondage), He called Abraham *from the East* (Gen. 12:1-3), over to the land of Canaan.

Bible chronologies and archaeology reveal that the false system of worship centered in Babylon was becoming a mighty force in the world while Abraham was growing into manhood. From this religious evil of the east, through which Satan aimed at world control, God called Abraham westward from the river Euphrates and the kingdom of Babylon (Josh. 24:2), in order that, through him, the true way of worship could be revealed.

In Old Testament times the dispensation of the literal operated. Babylon was then a *literal* city, but in the New Testament Babylon stands for a *spiritual* city, Rev. 14:8; etc. When east was mentioned *in relation to ancient Jerusalem and Babylon*, it referred to a literal east; but as those cities are spiritually applied in the Apocalypse, East, *when used in relation to them*, must also be spiritually applied. As I have shown in my "What Is Armageddon?", literal directions of the compass which at one time *related to the literal cities of Jerusalem and Babylon*, can only apply in the sense of an *imagery* when related to spiritual Jerusalem and Babylon. This law operates in the Scriptures until the millennium, which is an important key in the understanding of the prophecies. Failure to see that the literal east does not operate in this "dispensation of the Spirit" as it did in the Old Testament, when the sanctuary had to be erected *facing the east* (see Ex. 26:18, 20, 22, 35; Num. 2:3, 10, 18, 25), and the blood was to be sprinkled "upon the mercy seat *eastward*" (Lev. 16:14, 15) *made it easier for Sunday keeping to come into the Christian church,* as will be seen later in our study.

Today, when people come out of *spiritual* Babylon and go to *spiritual* Jerusalem they go from a spiritual east just as anciently God's people came out of literal Babylon situated to the east of Jerusalem. The literal in the Old Testament provides the *imagery* which is employed in the Apocalypse.

Babylon, where sun-worship was established, became the Biblical name for Satan's false system of worship. Jerusalem in the west "A city of truth" (Zech. 8:3), became the symbol of the true worship which is thus set in opposition to the erroneous system. Hence the Revelator refers to Christ's church as "*The Holy City.*" Rev. 11:2. The system furthering Satan's "self" principles is likewise called "*that great city* which reigneth over the kings of the earth," Rev. 17:18. "That great *city Babylon.*" Rev. 18:10. Thus, the same principles involved in ancient Babylon are to be the predominating religious influence till the second coming of Christ, when Babylon comes to a swift and an eternal end in the battle of Armageddon. In this connection the reader is urged to read Rev. 16:12-16, 19; 17:12-14; 19:11-21, and the eighteenth chapter of Revelation. Before the final, irretrievable destruction, Babylon, however, is predicted to make one more gigantic effort to dominate the world. As sin began so will it end—in self pretending to be engaged in the betterment of its fellows, while planning to destroy all who dare refuse its supremacy. Under the guise of a light-bearer, the almost universal "self"—the Babylonian world—will seek to crush others. Under a pretext of leading into light and liberty, self will yet endeavour to force all to pay homage. Lucifer's original motive of making himself supreme at all costs will be manifested in its worst form in sin's last desperate death struggle.

Chapter III

The Antiquity and Universality of Sun-worship

SUN-WORSHIP IN JOB'S DAY

The Book of Job, probably the first book of the Bible written, gives the history of the times between the flood and Moses. In its introduction, we observe that Job "in the land of Uz" "was the greatest of all the men of the east." Job 1:1-3. It was here that Satan struggled with Job over the supremacy of will. It was here that Job endured so much suffering at the hands of the evil one, who claimed lordship over the earth. Job 1:7; 2:1-7. It is in this Book that we find Satan's charge that God's servants serve Him for only selfish reasons. See Job 1:9; 2:4, 5.

In Job's day sun worship was already entrenched in the East. Hence we read in Job 31:26-28, "If I beheld *the sun* when it shined, or *the moon* walking in its brightness: and my heart hath been secretly enticed, or my mouth hath kissed my hand: This also were an iniquity to be punished by the Judge: *for I should have denied the God that is above.*"

Commenting on this passage, Calmet says:—"Job points out: I. The worship of the sun... much used in his time, and very anciently used in every part of the East.... II. The custom of adoring the sun at its rising."

Sun-worship was practiced by most of the eastern nations. Morer says:—"It is not to be denied that we borrow the *name* of this day (Sunday) from the ancient Greeks and Romans, and we allow that the old Egyptians worshipped the sun, and as a standing memorial of their veneration, *dedicated this day to him.*" *Dialogues on the Lord's Day*, p. 22.

The *Encyclopedia Britannica*, art. Baal, says:—"The Baal of the Syrians, Phoenicians, and heathen Hebrews is a much less elevated conception than the Babylon Bel. He is properly the sun-god, Baal-Shamen, Baal (Lord) of the heavens, the highest of the heavenly bodies."

SUN-WORSHIP AMONG THE EGYPTIANS

Prof. George Rawlinson says concerning sun-worship in Egypt: "Ra was the Egyptian sun-god, and was especially worshipped at Heliopolis (city of the sun).... The kings for the most part considered Ra their special patron and protector; nay, they went so far as to identify themselves with him, to use his titles as their own, and to adopt his name as the ordinary prefix to their own name and titles. This is believed by many to have been the origin of the word Pharaoh, which was, it is thought, the Hebrew rendering of Ph' Ra–'the sun.'" *Religions of the Ancient World*, p. 20.

Sun-worship with its satanic captivation, with its bewitching appeal to man's innate selfishness, quickly spread to the whole of the ancient world. Different names were used in different countries, and somewhat different ceremonies were employed, but it was everywhere the worship of the heavenly bodies. The sun was honoured whether known as Osiris, Atlas, Bacchus, Hercules, Orion, Mars, etc. The sun, the male deity, was first in the worship of the heavenly bodies, but, as a part of the same system came the moon—the female god—Beltis, Juno, Venus, Minerva, Rhea, etc. This iniquitous idolatry was not complete without the child of the gods—Apollo, Horus, Vishnu, Thor, Achilles, Zoroaster, Mithras, Cupid, Tammuz, etc.

"The universality of this form of idolatry," says Dr. Talbot W. Chambers, "is something remarkable. It seems to have prevailed everywhere."—*Old Testament Student*, January 1886.

SUN-WORSHIP AMONG THE PHOENICIANS

Of the Phoenicians, with whom the children of Israel were in close contact, we read:—

"The central point in religion, and the starting point in all Phoenician mythology, was the worship of the sun, who has either the moon or (as the sun is also the heaven god) the earth for wife.... In other places we find as spouse of the highest god, the moon goddess Astarte with the cow's horns, who in Tyre was worshipped under the symbol of a star as queen of heaven. With her worship, as with that of Baaltis, were associated wild orgies, and traces of the like are not lacking even at Carthage [Aug., Civ. Dei. ii. 4] where theology has given a more earnest and gloomy character to the goddess.... On account of his regular daily course the sun is viewed as the god who works and reveals himself in the world, as son of the god who is above the world, and as *protector* of civil order. But, again, as the sun engenders the fruitfulness of the earth, he becomes the object of a sensual nature worship one feature of which is that men and women interchange garments. A chief feast [similar to the festival of the Saxon goddess Eostre, from which comes our Easter] to his honor in Tyre was the 'awaking of Hercules' in the month Peritius [February and March], a festival of the returning power of the sun in spring." *Encyclopedia Britannica,* art., *'Phoenicia,'* vol. 18, pp. 802, 803 (9th ed.).

THE DEGRADATIONS OF SUN-WORSHIP

The worship of the sun was the most abominable and degrading of all idolatrous worship. It was often characterized by human sacrifices, by cutting and scourging, and by licentiousness that cannot be described.

Mosheim says of the heathen worship:—

"Their festivals and other solemn days were polluted by a licentious indulgence in every species of libidinous excess; and on these occasions they were not prohibited even from making the sacred mansions of the gods the scenes of vile and beastly gratification." *"Commentaries,"* introduction, chap. I, sec. II, edited by Murdock.

The antiquity of sun-worship is found in inscriptions on stones, in the temples that were dedicated to the sun in the early reigns of the kings of Assyria, Egypt, Babylon, and other nations of the east. Chaldea is doubtless the birthplace of sun-worship. Each nation has its own name for a sungod, as Molech, Baal, Chemosh, Baalzebub, Tammuz, Ra Apis, Osiris, and Isis, Jupiter, Apollo, etc., and each god had its female divinity. The student will encounter some difficulty in straightening out all the names—whether of the male, or female, or the child of the gods, according to the nation of origin and the time used in history—but such does not really matter as it was all sun-worship.

SUN-WORSHIP IN THE HINDU RELIGION

Sun-worship is a predominant feature of the Hindu religion under the name of Indra.

Olcott says, "The rising Sun was called *Brahma*; on the meridian it was known as *Siva*; and in the west at nightfall, *Vishnu*." Their morning prayer, facing the sun, is "Let us meditate on the desirable light of the divine Sun; may he rouse our minds." In Parsee temples fire worship is practiced.

From the pen of Alfred Koch we take the following:—

"In India from the earliest recorded time until today, sun worship has prevailed. Since the time of Veda, the sun has not ceased to predominate in the mythology as well as in the poetry and the religious literature of India.... We can perceive it even today in the daily religious ceremonies and festivals of the modern Hindu. Every morning we can see the Brahman, with his face directed toward the east, standing on one foot, stretching out both hands to the sun, as he recites the Gayatri, the old venerable formulas of prayer, 'Let's meditate about the welcome light of the godly sun; may he lift up our spirit.' This is, as one can see, a direct invoking of the sun.

"Sun worship prevails also among the Hindus of the Bombay district. The Brahmans regard the sun as their primary object of worship. Persons who desire the blessings of health, fortune, and happiness invoke the favor of the sun god, and for this purpose every Sunday they make a solemn vow in his honor. There are further found at different places in Bengal temples erected to the honor of the sun god. *Sunday is holy* to him, and on that day many abstain from eating fish or meat; in some districts people do not use salt on that day."

JAPAN AND SUN-WORSHIP

"In the national religion of Japan—Shintoism—sun worship has the most important place. Above all Shinto gods, the sun god—the personification of the real sun—is the dominant one. It is called *Amaterasu-no-Omikami*. The main place of worship of Amaterasu is at Ise.... It is the duty of every male Japanese if in any way possible, to go at least once in his life to Ise, and worship there.... Yet, many of the lower classes of the people, especially the women and the children, still believe the real sun to be the heavenly queen, called *O tento sama*. Standing upright, with hands laid together, and bowed heads, farmers and fishermen eagerly await the appearance of the sun, worshipping it either in silence or in a low voice...."

"Among the places of pilgrimage the tops of mountains are most esteemed, since the worshippers believe that they are closer to the heavenly gods, and from there the sun appears to be much larger than when viewed from a valley or from a plain. The Olympia of Japan, the Fujiyama, is ascended every summer by tens of thousands of pilgrims for the purpose of worship."

This able writer, in the series of articles which he wrote for an American journal, has shown the extensive nature of sun worship from the days of Babylon to our times.

Willard Price, in his *"Japan Reaches Out,"* has set aside chapter 33 to discuss "Japan's Divine Mission." Writing "of every child of the empire," the author says:—

"He grows up believing with every fibre of his being that:–

Japan is the only divine land.

Japan's Emperor is the only divine Emperor.

Japan's people are the only divine people.

Therefore, Japan must be the light of the world.

"Then as to the Emperor. The heavenly pair who begot the islands also gave birth to the Sun Goddess, Amaterasu, whose descendants ruled Japan.... But the Japanese divinity does not stop with the land and the Emperor. The people themselves partake of it. The earliest inhabitants of Japan were gods; and from them descended the present Yamato race, seed of the sun. All other mortals are of a lower order."

Sun-worship and self-exaltation have gone together, following the example of its author.

SUN-WORSHIP IN ISRAEL

Surrounded, as the Hebrews were, by whole nations of sun-worshippers, they were repeatedly led away from the true worship of God to that of idolatrous sun-worship, in the days of the Judges and the prophets. See Judges 2:11; 3:7; 6:25-32; 10:6; Ps. 106:35, 36; I Kings 12:26-31; 18:17-26; II Kings 10:29; 21:1-7, etc.

Sun-worship was so strong and so baleful upon the whole of mankind that God, through the writers of the Bible, frequently commanded His people to turn from everything associated with it. The Israelites were forbidden to cut their hair to resemble the disc and the rays of the sun, as did the sun-worshippers. Lev. 19:27. They were explicitly enjoined not to make the images which were a part of this paganism. In fact, they were to destroy these images, and were to refrain from anything that was associated with sun-worship. Deut. 4:15-19; 17:2-5; Ex. 23:24; Lev. 26:1; Deut. 7:5; II Kings 18:4.

It is a significant fact that whenever the Israelites forsook God's worship they immediately joined themselves to sun-worship. Judges 2:11-13; etc., I Kings 16:31-34.

In II Kings 23:1-20 is chronicled the work of the good king Josiah in reforming Israel by destroying the sun-worshipping system, which had plagued the Israelites and turned them from God. Though repeatedly purged from this God-dishonouring cult by men of God's appointment, the Jews became more and more given over to it, until, at the time of their Babylonian captivity, they were wholly under its pernicious influence. In Jer. 7:9-18 we read God's lament over the apostacy of His people. There were men, women and children engaged in making "cakes"—hot cross buns—"to the queen of heaven." Visions were given to Ezekiel revealing that the entire nation through its representatives had gone into this Satan-planned religion. "There sat women weeping for Tammuz." Ezek. 8:14. Some of these pagan customs are still perpetuated within the Christian church.

"Then said He unto me, Hast thou seen this O son of man? Turn thee yet again, and thou shalt see greater abominations than these. And He brought me into the inner court of the Lord's house, and, behold, at the door of the temple of the Lord, between the porch and the altar, were about five and twenty men, with *their backs toward the temple* of the Lord and their *faces toward the east*; and they *worshipped the sun toward the east*." Ezek. 8:16.

One reason why God had ordered His tabernacle in the wilderness to be built facing the east, was so that those who came to worship Him would always have their backs to the east or the *rising* sun. To worship the rising sun (an important feature of sun-worship), therefore, meant to turn one's back upon the Lord. See Ex. 26:18, 20, 22, 36; Ezek. 8:16.

The twenty-five men Ezekiel saw worshipping with their backs to the temple of the Lord, were the High Priest and his twenty-four associate priests, who worked in the temple in courses of twenty-four. See I Chron. 24:5-19; 25:7-31; Rev. 4:4, 10; 5:8, 14, etc.

That the people of the Jewish nation should have gone over to the worship of the sun at all is astonishing, but to have the priesthood leading the nation in its worship is most remarkable, especially in view of the Divine prohibitions in connection therewith. It was forbidden by the Lord under sentence of death. Deut. 4:19; 13:6-11; 18:9-14. The priests were not to mar their beards, or to make bald the crown of the head, as did the heathen sun priests. They were not to do penance by cutting themselves, as did the priests of the sun, nor prostitute their daughters, as did the devotees of this abominable idolatry. Compare Lev. 19:28, 29 with I Kings 18:26, 28. Neither were God's people to observe the "times" of the heathen. Lev. 19:26; Deut. 18:10, 11; Lev. 19:30, 27. Yet, despite such stern denunciations from the Almighty, Israel went after the idols of the heathen around them. They forsook the pure fountain of life, and drank of the polluted waters of idolatry. But, as we shall show, Israel's acceptance of sun-worshipping customs is duplicated in the Christian church. Such is the power of Satan. Israel "mingled among the heathen, and learned their works. And they served *their idols*: which were a snare unto them. Yea, they sacrificed their sons and their daughters unto devils." Ps. 106:35-37. This truth is repeated by the Inspired Paul, "But I say, that the things which the Gentiles sacrifice, they sacrifice to *devils*, and not to God: and I would not that ye should have fellowship *with devils*." I Cor. 10:20. Sun-worship, with all of its ramifications, is declared by God to be devil-worship—it is carrying out the principles which entered into Lucifer's heart when he rebelled against God and introduced the frightful woes which have befallen the human family.

To get a more adequate picture of the incalculable hypnotic power of this devil-inspired system we will show how it has even entered into the sacred confines of God's organization—the church—which was ordained by its Founder to oppose Satan's work upon earth. When the Israelites failed in this task, the church was set apart to oppose Satan's system. But, as Israel absorbed and fell before the very thing it was ordained to defeat, so the church has largely fallen a prey to the designs of God's enemy. Many customs which are practiced in the Christian church to-day had their origin in sun-worship—customs which were hoary with age when Jesus was born, and opposed to God's work in the times of the Old Testament, wherein they are condemned.

CHAPTER IV

THE ORIGIN OF CHRISTMAS DAY —THE BIRTHDAY OF THE SUN

My deep sympathies are with those who have reverently looked upon Christmas as Christ's birthday. In all sincerity and innocence they have had special regard for this day. It may come as somewhat of a surprise, and even shock, to be told that whatever date Jesus was born upon, it certainly could not have been December 25th. As gently as he can say it the writer says, "Christmas Day is not Christ's birthday."

From the *Melbourne Herald*, of Dec. 21/28 we quote:—

"Christmas Day has not always been kept on a fixed day, for at first it was as much a moveable feast as Easter, and was celebrated by the Eastern churches in April and May.... The Egyptians held that it fell in January, according to the old style of reckoning. Russia, under the rule of the Czars, adhered to the old style, and held her Christmas festival in January. Others placed it in June, and others again held that Christ's birth happened in July. At one period, December 6 was declared to be the proper anniversary, and the feast was celebrated at Cypress on that day as early as the fourth century. For one or two centuries, the Eastern churches observed Christmas Day on January 6, and it was only after a considerable lapse of time that a general agreement was come to in favour of December 25."

In the *Calcutta (India) Statesman*, December 1922, appeared a lengthy exposition of "the origin of Christmas Day," giving a "history of the greatest festival of the Christian year."

"Is the 25th of December really the day on which our Saviour first showed Himself in human form in the manger at Bethlehem?... In the earliest periods at which we have any record of the observance of Christmas, we find some communities of

Christians celebrated the festival on January 1 or 6; others on March 29, the time of the Jewish Passover; while others, it is said, observed it on September 29, or Feast of Tabernacles.... The custom of the Western church at last prevailed, and both of the ecclesiastical bodies [Eastern and Western] agreed to hold the anniversary on the same day. The fixing of the date appears to have been the act of Julius I, who presided as pope or bishop of Rome, from 337 to 352 A.D....

"Though Christian nations have thus, from an early period in the history of the church, celebrated Christmas about the period of the winter solstice, or the shortest day, it is well known that many, and, indeed, the greater number of the popular festive observances by which it is characterized, are traceable to a much more ancient origin. Amid *all* the pagan nations of antiquity, there seems to have been a universal tendency *to worship the sun as the giver of life and light,* and the visible manifestation of the Deity.

"By the Romans, this anniversary was celebrated under the title of Saturnalia, or the festival of Saturn, and was marked by the prevalence of a universal license and merrymaking....

"In the early stages of Christianity, its ministers frequently experienced the utmost difficulty in inducing the converts to refrain from indulging in the popular amusements which were so largely participated in by their pagan countrymen. Among others, the revelry and license which characterized the Saturnalia called for special animadversion. But at last, convinced partly of the inefficacy of such denunciations, and partly influenced by the idea that the spread of Christianity might thereby be advanced, the church endeavoured to amalgamate, as it were, the old and the new religions, and sought by transferring the heathen ceremonies to the solemnities of the Christian festivals, to make them subservient to the cause of religion and piety.... The result has been the strange medley of Christian and pagan rites which contribute to make up the festivities of the modern Christmas."

Another authority says:—

"Regarding Christmas, the holiday universally celebrated in honour of the birth of Christ, we must say that whatever may have been the date of our Saviour's birth, it is certain that it could not have been December 25, at which time of the year the shepherds of Palestine would not think of abiding with their flocks in the field. The day of the birth of Jesus has been guessed at by many writers. His birthday has been placed in every month of the year. The Egyptians placed it in January; Bochart prefers March; some mentioned by Clemens Alexandrinus argue for April, others for May. Epiphanius speaks of some who placed it in June, and of others who have supposed it to have been in July. Wagenseil thinks it was probably in August; Lightfoot on the 15th of September; Scaliger, Casaubon, and Calvisius, in October, others in November. But the Roman Church, claiming to be supreme in power and infallible in judgment, has declared the date to be December 25, the very day on which the ancient Romans celebrated the feast of their goddess, Bruma."

See also note on Luke 2:8 from the pen of *Dr. Adam Clarke*, the famous Methodist commentator.

The Editor of the *Christchurch Press*, December 24/25, wrote:—

"Whatever Christians thought once they know now that shepherds would not be watching their flocks by night in the middle of Palestine's rainy season. They know also that the early Christians kept the festival in three different months, and that it was partly at least *under Pagan influences* that believers agreed at last to be joyful towards the end of December.... For in the Northern World they have come to the winter solstice, *which mankind celebrated long before the birth of Christ*, because the nights began to decrease then and the days to increase, and hope was born again and the blackest days had passed."

Not only secular writers have shown the widespread knowledge of the sun-worshipping origin of Christmas day, for church authorities have made no endeavour to hide the fact that December 25th was not the birthday of Jesus.

The Rev. Canon R. H. Murray, Litt.D., writing in the *Contemporary Review* for December, 1921, says:—

"That He [Christ] was born is true, that He was born on December 25 is false. The reasons against this date are overwhelming. The shepherds in remote places used to take out their flocks in March and bring them home in November, not December."

Many great Bible scholars such as Doddridge (author of "Rock of Ages"), Joseph Mede, Lightfoot, Joseph Scaliger, Jennings (in his *Jewish Antiquities*), and many others, have long since pointed out that December 25 could not possibly have been the date of the Saviour's birth.

Dr. Albert Barnes, the noted Presbyterian commentator, in his remarks on Luke 2:8, says:—

"It is also a fact that the Jews sent out their flocks into the mountains and desert regions during the summer months, and took them up in the latter part of October or the first of November, when the cold weather commenced.... It is clear from this that our

Saviour was born before the 25th of December, or before what we call Christmas. At that time it is cold, and especially in the high and mountainous regions about Bethlehem. God has concealed the time of His birth. There is no way to ascertain it. By different men it has been fixed at each month in the year. Nor was it of consequence to know the time; if it had been, God would have preserved the record of it."

Says the Rev. Alexander Hislop:—

"Long before the fourth century, and *long before the Christian era itself*, a festival was celebrated among the *heathen*, at that precise time of the year (December 25) in honour of *the birth of the son of the Babylonian queen of heaven.*

"That Christmas was originally a pagan festival is beyond all doubt. The time of the year, and the ceremonies with which it is still celebrated, prove its origin.... The very name by which Christmas is popularly known among ourselves—Yule-day—proves at once its pagan and Babylonian origin. 'Yule' is the Chaldee name for 'infant' or 'little child'; and as the 25th of December was called by our pagan Anglo-Saxon ancestors, 'Yule-day,' or the 'Child's day,' long before they came in contact with Christianity, that sufficiently proves its real character. Far and wide, in the realms of paganism, was this birthday observed." *The Two Babylons*, page 93, etc.

This learned church author traces most of the Christmas customs to the sun-worshipping pagans. If he has not already done so, the reader is advised to read all that the Rev. Hislop has written on this subject.

The ancients regarded December 25, Christmas Day, as the *birthday* of the *Sun*. It is certainly *not* the birthday of "the Sun of Righteousness" (Mal. 4:2).

Lucifer, the "Day Star," has bewitched people to honour him by honouring the day of which he is the author.

In the Christmas festival, the church faces the sun.

CHAPTER V

THE ORIGIN OF EASTER

In observing the Easter services, many honest-hearted Christians believe that they celebrate a divinely-appointed Church festival in commemoration of the death and the resurrection of Christ Jesus, the Lord. Not so, however. In the first place, the Easter festival is a moveable one; and a *shifting* date, dependant upon the phases of the moon, can never logically be the anniversary of the event which definitely occurred on a *definite* date nearly two thousand years ago. The date of a man's birth is fixed; it must always be a certain date of a certain month. So it should be with the anniversary of Christ's resurrection were it necessary to celebrate it in this fashion. The Lord's supper, however, instituted by Christ Himself, is the Bible practice of commemorating Christ's crucifixion and death; while baptism by immersion is the God-appointed ceremony of reminding us of Christ's resurrection. See Rom. 6:3-5; Col. 2:12. This is a daily memorial, for, as the believer endeavours to walk each day "in newness of life" he experiences Christ's resurrection power, and the Lord's death and resurrection are remembered daily.

As to the popular manner of celebrating Easter, we learn from history that not only is this Easter festival a tree with pagan roots, but that much of its fruit, as seen in the prevailing customs, is also pagan.

This statement is supported by an article in the *Melbourne Herald* of April, 19/1919:—

> "The festival of Easter... replaced a pagan festival originally held in Great Britain in honour of Eostre, the Anglo-Saxon goddess

of spring, after whom the festival was named. This in turn had followed the forms and rites of festivals which had been practiced by the ancient Greeks, Phoenicians, Syrians, and Egyptians *in honour of their solar deity* known under the names of Adonis, Dionysus, Tammuz, Krishna, etc."

This pagan ceremony was worked into the early Christian Church, says the ecclesiastical historian Socrates, by claiming it to be "the perpetuation of an old usage, just as many other customs were established."

In other words, the introduction of these heathen customs into the Church was nothing but a bribe to gain converts—a compromise with Satan.

The Rev. Alexander Hislop writes:—"What means the term Easter? It is not a Christian name. It bears its Chaldean origin on its very forehead. Easter is nothing less than Astarte, one of the titles of Beltis, the queen of heaven." *The Two Babylons*, p.103.

The Easter season was certainly not originated by our Lord or His apostles, or by any of the other earlier leaders of the church of Jesus Christ; it has crept into Christendom from sources that had nothing to do with Christianity. It cannot in any sense be called a true Christian institution. The origin of the term is found in ancient Chaldean pagan worship. Easter and Astarte are one and the same; and Astarte was one of the titles of Beltis, whom the pagans honoured as the queen of heaven. In Ninevah the name was pronounced Ishtar. The worship of Ishtar, or Astarte, or Beltis, was early introduced into Britain, along with the Druids, "the prophets of the groves" referred to in the Bible. See I Kings 18:19. The worship of Ishtar was a species of sun worship, or worship of the heavenly bodies, so strictly forbidden by the God of heaven through his prophets. Many Christians, not knowing the origin of Easter, and not knowing that it has nothing whatever to do with Christianity, take part in its celebration, thinking that in so doing they are honouring their risen Lord. That the "sins of their ignorance" God may "wink at" or pass over without chastisement, does not free us, when we know better, from our obligation to observe only what God Himself has commanded or established—especially when we profess to be doing these things in His honour.

THE ORIGIN OF LENT

The Rev. Alexander Hislop in his *Two Babylons*, writes concerning Lent and Easter:—

"Whence, then, came this observance? The forty days abstinence of Lent was directly borrowed from the worshippers of the Babylonian goddess. Such a Lent of forty days, 'in the spring of the year,' is still observed by the Yezidis, or pagan devil-worshippers of Kurdistan, who have inherited it from their early masters, the Babylonians. Such a Lent of forty days was held in the spring by the pagan Mexicans, for thus we read in Humboldt, where he gives an account of Mexican observances:—'Three days after the vernal equinox... began a solemn fast of forty days in *honour of the sun.*' Such a Lent of forty days was observed in Egypt, as may be seen on consulting Wilkinson's 'Egyptians.' This Egyptian Lent of forty days, we are informed by Landseer, in his 'Sabean Researches,' was held expressly in commemoration of Adonis or Osiris.

"Among the pagans this Lent seems to have been an indispensable preliminary to the great annual festival in commemoration of the death and resurrection of Tammuz, which was celebrated by alternate weeping and rejoicing, and, which, in many countries, was considerably later than the Christian festival, being observed in Palestine and Assyria in June, therefore called the 'month of Tammuz'.... To conciliate the pagans to nominal Christianity, Rome, pursuing its usual policy, took measures to get the Christian and pagan festivals amalgamated, and by a complicated but skilful adjustment of the calendar, it was found no difficult matter, in general, to get paganism and Christianity—now sunk in idolatry—in this as in so many other things, to shake hands....

"This change of the calendar in regard to Easter was attended with momentous consequences. It brought into the church the grossest corruption and the rankest superstition in connection with the abstinence of lent...."

"The difference, in point of time, betwixt the Christian Pasch, as observed in Britain by the native Christians, and the pagan Easter enforced by Rome, at the time of its enforcement, was a whole month; and it was only by violence and bloodshed at last that the festival of the Anglo-Saxon or Chaldean goddess came to supersede that which had been held in honour of Christ." *Two Babylons*, pp. 103-107.

Here then, is an institution which has never had divine sanction, had no divine appointment, was objected to by native

Christians at the time of its enforcement, was resisted, and was enforced finally only through persecution and bloodshed. Can it, then, be said that the Christian Church does well in its observance? Can we take our religious observances from paganism, and please God in so doing? Can that religious observance unauthorized by God, and which was enforced by fear and bloodshed, be accepted by our Farther as a humble, free-will offering from His own children? What God condemned anciently, He does not bless today.

In the days of Ezekiel God showed him certain abominations which His people were committing. Abomination after abomination was shown the prophet, and then the Lord said: "Turn thee yet again, and thou shalt see *greater* abominations that they do. Then He brought me to the door of the gate of the Lord's house which was toward the north; and, behold, there sat women weeping for Tammuz." Ezek. 8:13, 14. Now Tammuz was the lover, or husband, of Ishtar (Astarte, Easter), the goddess of heaven. Her lover, according to this pagan myth, was slain in the summer, and was resurrected to life again. The women, in this system of pagan worship, would first weep for the death of Tammuz, and then rejoice over his resurrection. Thus, this weeping of the women of Israel, which the Lord pointed out to His prophet, showed that they who were so doing had apostatized from the worship of the true God and were worshipping Ishtar (Astarte, or Easter). God condemned them for this apostasy, and declared it to be a great abomination. So the whole season of Lent and Easter is branded by the Word of God as apostasy and displeasing to Him, and is condemned by Him.

WHY DYED EGGS AND EASTER RABBITS?

Have you ever wondered why the children play with dyed eggs and Easter rabbits on a day supposedly set aside to honour the resurrection of Jesus? It is a paradox. Easter rabbits and dyed eggs were the definite signs of returning life from the queen of heaven. The egg was used as a symbol of fertility, or life, while the rabbit was a token of reproduction and germination.

From the magazine, *The Pathfinder*, March 30, 1929, we quote:—

"Most people know that Easter is celebrated in memory of the crucifixion and resurrection of our Saviour. But few realize that it had a heathen origin. This festival was in honour of Eostre or Easter.... All youngsters are fascinated with the seasonal rabbits and eggs. The Easter egg and the legend of the rabbit are universal. The egg was the pagan emblem of germinating life in early spring. The rabbit is another pagan symbol and has always been an emblem of fertility."

THE HOT-CROSS BUN

Concerning Easter buns and eggs, Hislop says:—

"The hot cross buns of Good Friday, and the dyed eggs of Pasch or Easter Sunday, *figured in the Chaldean rites just as they do now*. The 'buns' known too by that identical name, were used in the worship of the queen of heaven, the goddess of Easter, as early as Cecrops, the founder of Athens—that is, 1,500 years before the Christian era." *The Two Babylons*, p. 108.

"The origin of the Pasch eggs is just as clear. The ancient Druids bore an egg, as the sacred emblem of their order.... The Hindoo fables celebrate their sacred egg as of golden colour. The people of Japan make their sacred egg to have been brazen. In China, at this hour, dyed or painted eggs are used on sacred festivals. In ancient times eggs were used in religious rites of the Egyptians and the Greeks, and were hung up for mystic purposes in their temples. From Egypt these sacred eggs can be distinctly traced to the banks of the Euphrates.... An egg of wondrous size is said to have fallen from heaven into the river Euphrates. The fishes rolled it to the bank, where the doves having settled upon it, and hatched it, out came Venus, who afterwards was called the Syrian Goddess—that is, Astarte. Hence the egg became one of the symbols of Astarte or Easter.... The Romish church adopted this mystic egg of Astarte, and consecrated it as a symbol of the resurrection of Christ....

"Astarte… was worshipped not only as an incarnation of the Spirit of God, but also of the mother of mankind." *The Two Babylons*, pp. 108-111.

Extracts from many more authorities regarding the origin and customs of Easter could be quoted, but let this article from the *Melbourne Sun*, April 11, 1925, suffice. It is a talk to children and its simplicity appeals to us.

"Have you ever thought of the origin of Easter? The word has undoubtedly something to do with the east. It was *in the East* where the word had its origin, and, of course, the festival, as we observe it, relates to something that, from our point of the compass, happened in the East. But long before the great event which we commemorate at this season occurred, eggs seem to have had a part in the ceremonies that then took place. As we recognize Easter it is, of course, a Christian festival, but there was a time when it was a festival of a very different kind. The old Babylonians knew a great deal about it. So did the ancient Egyptians. So, too, did our remote forefathers in the days when they are said to have painted their bodies and protected themselves from the cold of winter by wrapping the skins of beasts around them."

After giving the origin of Easter from Astarte the article continues:—

"And from whence springs the hot-cross bun customs? Some authorities trace the hot-cross bun back as far as pagan times. The ancient Greeks worshipped the moon-goddess with cakes which they marked with a cross, thought to refer to four quarters of the moon. And here we have a fresh story, which holds that it was to honour Eostra—the goddess of Spring—the pagan Saxons ate cross-bread. Bakers in England in the 13th century were forbidden by royal proclamation to mark their bread and buns with a cross."

Hundreds of years before Christ's death on the cross, apostate Israel made hot-cross buns to the queen of heaven. Jer. 7:9-18.

THE CROSS

Concerning the sign of the cross, history reveals that it was used thousands of years before the crucifixion of Jesus. It came from the Tau of Chaldeans and Egyptians—the initial T in the name of the god, Tammuz. Priests of sun-worship bore it on their person, and the vestal virgins of pagan Rome wore it about their necks. In the *Edinburgh Review,* October, 1870, we read concerning the pre-Christian cross:—

"From the dawn of organized paganism in the Eastern world, to the final establishment of Christianity in the Western, the cross was undoubtedly the commonest and most sacred of symbolical monuments, and to a remarkable extent it is so still in almost every land where that of Calvary is unrecognized or unknown."

And again from Wilson W. Blake, we read, "The cross and the crescent were combined in the Oriental standards centuries before the time of Christ," *The Cross, Ancient and Modern.*

While to many Christians the cross on the church, or the crucifix worn or carried, is the symbol of the death of Christ—the sun-worshippers carried and used this emblem for millenniums before Christ. As Dr. Inman has said, "The devout Christian believes that all who venerate the cross may hope for a happy eternity, without ever dreaming that the sign of his faith is as ancient as Homeric Troy, and was used by the Phoenicians probably before the Jews had any existence as a people."

The Rev. Alexander Hislop, in his *Two Babylons*, has gone into this matter extensively, and concerning the origin and significance of the cross, he says:—

> "In the Papal system, as is well known, the sign of the cross and the image of the cross are all in all. No prayer can be said, no worship engaged in, no step almost can be taken, without the frequent use of the sign of the cross.... The same sign of the cross that Rome now worships was used in Babylonian mysteries, was applied to the same magic purposes, was honoured with the same honours. That which is now called the Christian cross was originally no Christian emblem at all, but was the mystic Tau of the Chaldeans and Egyptians—the true original form of the letter T—the initial of the name Tammuz.... That mystic Tau was marked in baptism on the foreheads of those initiated into the Mysteries, and was used in every variety of way as a most sacred symbol. To identify Tammuz with the sun it was joined sometimes to the circle of the sun, sometimes it was *inserted* in the circle.... Maltese cross is an express symbol of the sun.... The mystic Tau, as the symbol of the great divinity, was called 'the sign of life'; it was used as an amulet over the heart; it was marked on the official garments of the priests, as on the official garments on the priests of Rome.... The vestal virgins of Pagan Rome wore it suspended from their necklaces, as the nuns do now. The Egyptians did the same, and many of the barbarous nations with whom they had intercourse, as the Egyptian monuments bear witness... showing that it was already in use *as early as the fifteenth century before the Christian era*. There is hardly a Pagan tribe where the cross has not been found. The cross was worshipped by the Pagan Celts long before the incarnation and death of Christ.... The cross thus widely worshipped, or regarded as a sacred emblem, was the unequivocal symbol of Bacchus, the Babylonian Messiah, for he was represented with a head-band covered with crosses." *The Two Babylons*, pp. 197-199.

Many church festivals and ceremonies are undoubtedly of sun-worshipping origin. *Olcott*, in his *Sun Lore of All Ages* says:—

> "In short, sun-worship, symbolically speaking, *lies at the heart of the great festivals* which the Christian church celebrates today, and these relics of *heathen religion* have, through the medium of

their sacred rites, curiously enough blended with practices and beliefs utterly antagonistic to the spirit that prompted them."

The doctrines of sun-worship, against which God had always warned his followers, were interwoven into the teachings of the true faith until the whole was a compromise. In many ways the church faces the rising sun.

EASTER AND SUNDAY EXALTATION

In the early centuries of the Christian era, in the days of apostasy in the professing Christian church, the Easter services were arranged so that the supposed resurrection day would serve to exalt *Sunday* observance. Fixed annual events, like our birthdays, should go through the days of the week. December 25, each year, falls upon a different *day* of the *week*. But the remarkable thing is that, while Christ's supposed *birthday* falls upon a *different day* each year, yet *His death* and *resurrection* days are fixed to come on the *same days* every year!

Obviously, this is an impossibility in actual fact. But if something had not been done to interfere with the annual cycle, Christ's death, like His birth, would fall upon a different day of the week each year. That would not have mattered, surely! But this natural sequence would have opened the eyes of many each year to the obvious fact that, as the day commemorating Christ's resurrection is an annual event, and falling upon a different day of the week each year, then *Sunday*, the first day of the week, *would have no special significance* when observed in honour of His resurrection. But why thrust aside the positive Commandment to keep the Seventh-day Sabbath in order to honour Christ's resurrection? Christ's death was prefigured each year in the Mosaic regime by the death of the passover Lamb on the 14th day of the 1st month. His resurrection was foreshadowed annually by the waving of the First Fruits on the 16th day of the 1st month. Thus, *if* it were God's plan for us to honour Christ's resurrection day it would have been, as in the type, an *annual* event. But, falling upon a different day of the week each year, it would not have added any holiness, or significance to the different days of the *week* it fell upon, for it would synchronize with them all in their turn.

The International Standard Bible Encyclopedia, under "Easter," says, —

"The English word comes from 'Eastre or Estera,' a teutonic goddess to whom sacrifice was offered in April, so the name was transferred to the Paschal feast.... Differences arose as to the time of the Easter celebrations; the *Jewish* Christians naturally fixing it at the time of the Paschal feast which was regulated by the paschal moon. According to this reckoning it began on the evening of the 14ᵗʰ day of the month Nisan *without regard to the day of the week*, while the *Gentile* Christians identified it with the first day of the week, i.e., the Sunday of the resurrection, irrespective of the month."

In his *The History of the Popes*, vol. 1, p. 18, Bower says:—

"But what most of all distinguished the pontificate of Victor was the famous controversy about the celebration of Easter between the Eastern and Western Bishops; the former keeping that solemnity on the 14ᵗʰ day of the first moon, on *what day soever it happened to fall*; and the latter putting it off till the Sunday following.... Victor, not satisfied with what his predecessors had done, took upon himself to impose the Roman custom on all the churches that followed the contrary practice. But in this bold attempt, which we may call the first essay of papal usurpation, he met with a vigorous and truly Christian opposition."

Truly, as Bower says, this endeavour to force all the churches to celebrate the Easter services so that the resurrection day would come every year on a *Sunday* (so as to exalt Sunday) was "the first essay of papal usurpation."

The apostate church very soon arranged matters so that the annual services to commemorate the death and resurrection of Christ were fixed to fall every year on Friday and Sun-day, respectively. And, as we have seen in Hislop's *Two Babylons*, the time of the celebration of Easter was enforced in Britain by "violence and bloodshed." Satan has always exalted his sun-days—whether annual (Christmas Day), or weekly (Sunday). The weekly festival, of course, is the chief festival which he seeks to exalt, because it is in direct opposition to God's explicitly-stated Commandment to keep holy the Seventh-day Sabbath.

In "the final conflict" the contest will be over God's Sabbath, His sign, or seal (Ezek. 20:12, 20; Rev. 7:1-4). This is the sign by which God knows that those who honour it humbly bow before His will, and have laid down their own wills upon His altar.

Satan, on the other hand, will strive to persuade the world to render obedience to his will in the observance of his weekly Sun-day, the first day of the week, which will *then* be "the mark of the beast." See Revelation, chapters 13-19.

CHAPTER VI

The Invincible Sun God Versus
the Invincible Son of God

THE SUN GOD RULED THE EARTH!

Notice the following extract from an authoritative source:—

"In the earliest forms of religious worship the sun held a prominent position.... The old Ayran tribes, the ancient Persians, the Brahmans of India, and the Pueblo Indians of North America, especially Mexico, all held to the belief that the *sun* and its companion, the *moon*, were *the great rulers of the earth*. In Egypt, sun worship was carried to a great extent into the mythology of the nation. In Mexico the Spanish conquerors found a people whose largest temples were dedicated to the Sun, and *whose every acts were guided by the priests of the sun.*"—*Encyclopedia Britannica* 20th Cent. Ed., vol. 29, pp. 196, 197.

SATAN, THE SUN GOD, TAKES THE PLACE
OF JESUS, THE TRUE GOD

"The sun, as the great source of light and heat, was worshipped under the name of Baal. Now, the fact that the sun, under that name, was worshipped in the earliest ages of the world, shows *the audacious character of these first beginnings of apostasy.* Men have spoken as if the worship of the sun and other heavenly bodies was an excusable thing into which the human race might very readily and very innocently fall—but how stands the fact?

"According to the primitive language of mankind, the sun was called 'Shemesh'—that is, 'the servant,'—that name, no doubt, being divinely given to keep the world in mind of the great truth that, however glorious the orb of day, it was after all, the appointed *minister* to the bounty of the great unseen Creator to His creatures upon earth. Men knew this, and yet, with the full knowledge of it, *they put the servant in the place of the Master, and called the sun*

41

Baal, that is, the Lord—and worshipped him accordingly. What a meaning, then, in the saying of Paul, that, when they knew God, they glorified Him not as God, but 'changed the truth of God into a lie, and worshipped and served the creature more than the Creator, who is God over all, blessed forever.' *The beginning, then, of Sun worship and of the worship of the host of heaven, was a sin against the light—a presumptuous, heaven-daring sin."* The Two Babylons, Rev. Alexander Hislop, p. 226, 7th Edition.

THE INVINCIBLE SUN GOD

Invincibility was ascribed to the sun by its devotees. The title universally applied to the sun god was "The Invincible Sun." And, surely, as we see the vast influence which this system has exerted upon mankind, we cannot help but admit that some mighty power has promulgated and supported it. How indelibly stamped upon the mind of man—how imperishable its institutions and festivals, that even the Christian church bows before the majesty of the sun god.

The *Schaff-Herzog Encyclopedia*, Art. "Sun," says:—

"The sun was worshipped among the Persians under the form of Mithras, which finally became the Sol Deus Invictus (*the invincible sun god*) throughout the West, especially through the Romans."

Throughout the East sun-worship was practiced under many names, but when sun-worship invaded Rome it was known as Mithraism. It spread rapidly, and by the "middle of the third century (A.D.) Mithraism seemed on the verge of becoming the universal religion."

"Sun-worship was so firmly entrenched in Rome that when Diocletian ascended the throne in A.D. 284, he took before the army an oath to the sun, declaring himself innocent of slaying the former Emperor."—*Decline and Fall of the Roman Empire*, chapter 12, page 71.

By the time of Constantine things had begun to change. Christianity was making itself felt. Nevertheless, Constantine "persevered till he was nearly forty years of age in the practice of the established religion." "His liberality restored and enriched the temples of the gods.... But the devotion of Constantine was more peculiarly directed to the genius of the sun, the Apollo of Greek and Roman mythology.... The sun was *universally celebrated as the invincible guide* and protector of Constantine." *Decline and Fall of the Roman Empire*, by Gibbon, chapter 20, page 3.

Constantine caused, during the first quarter of his reign, the minting of many coins with figures or busts of the sun god, and above it, or below it, he put the words, "*To the unconquered sun*," or "*To the unconquered sun*, the companion of Augustus."

Even in the year of 354 A.D. games were played in the circus at Rome in honour of "the unconquered sun."

Writing of the origin of the Christmas tree, Hislop says:—

"The Christmas tree, now so common among us, was equally common in Pagan Rome and Pagan Egypt. In Egypt it was the palm-tree; in Rome it was the fir; the palm-tree denoting the Pagan Messiah, as Baal-Tamar, the fir referring to him as Baal-Berith. The mother of Adonis, the Sun-God and great mediatorial divinity, was mystically said to have changed into a tree, and when in that state to have brought forth her divine son… the divine child born at the winter solstice was born as a new incarnation of the great god (after that god had been cut in pieces).... Now the great god, cut off in the midst of his power and glory, was symbolized as a huge tree, stripped of all its branches, and cut down almost to the ground. But *the great serpent, the symbol of the life restoring Aesculapius*, twists itself around the dead stock, and lo, at its side up sprouts a young tree—a tree of an entirely different kind, that is destined never to be cut down by hostile power… the Christmas tree… covertly symbolized the new-born God as Baal-Berith, 'Lord of the Covenant,' and thus shadowed forth the perpetuity and everlasting nature of his power, now that after having fallen before his enemies, he had risen triumphant over them all. Therefore, the 25th of December, the day that was observed at Rome as the day when the victorious god reappeared on earth, was held as the *Natalis invicti solis, 'The birth-day of the unconquered Sun'*… the Christmas tree is Nimrod *redivius*—the slain god come to life." *The Two Babylons*, pp. 97, 98.

Here we see that "that old serpent, called the Devil, and Satan, which deceiveth the whole world" (Rev. 12:9) is blasphemously represented as the life-giver, through whom victory is assured. In every way possible Satan has counterfeited the things of God and put himself in the place of the Lord.

Notice the following extract from an article—"The Master Counterfeiter"—written by Murl Vance:—

"A peculiarity, however, soon appears in these multitudinous manifestations of the sun-god. Almost invariably, *no matter where we find sun worship* on the face of the earth, either ancient or modern, we find a *sacred serpent accompanying such worship*. Take ancient Egypt, for instance. On Egyptian inscriptions we find the sun always pictured in the sky encircled by the cobra. The cobra, likewise, is pictured as being a part of the headdress of the queen and of the Pharaoh, who was deified as the sun-god on earth. We also find the sun temples everywhere containing their sacred serpent.

"This holds true likewise among both ancient and modern Indians of America, and among the most savage tribes of Africa, the Orient, or the islands of the sea. Everywhere the sun-god is accompanied by his sacred serpent. Why? Can it be that back in the cradle of sun worship, in ancient Babylon, the serpent meant more to the apostate worshippers than merely an earthly reptile? Fortunately for the student desiring an answer to such a question, various scientific organizations have recovered and translated thousands of the clay Babylonian temple texts, so that anyone who desires can read these strange facts in his own language.

WHEN THE DEVIL MADE HIMSELF GOD

"That the devil himself, not the sun, should become the real deity of paganism, at first seems almost unbelievable; but such proves to be the case. The reason for such devil worship soon becomes apparent when one interviews the modern followers of this ancient religion. Worship, they declare, has no other object than to appease the evil spirits. A good being needs no appeasing—he is naturally kind and good. It is the evil one that man must fear; worship him, and he will bless you and give fortune in place of misfortune. That the conclusion is not true is evident when one observes the degraded, superstitious, fear-crazed followers of devil worship today; but at any rate the reasoning must have sounded fairly plausible to the ancients who turned their back upon God and accepted Lucifer as their deity.

"That the sun as an object of worship is merely considered as a visible manifestation of Satan by so-called sun worshippers becomes at once apparent when one examines the titles by which the sun-god is addressed. Here are a few of them, taken primarily from the translations of Babylonian temple texts by Jastrow and Sayce: 'Lord of the lower world,' 'sword,' 'god of fire,' 'raging king,' 'the violent one,' 'the one that lies in wait,' 'the oppressor,' 'the soul of the sun,' 'the spy,' 'prince of Hades,' 'the ruler over the great city' [Babylon?], 'the lightning flash,' 'the plague demon,' 'the serpent,' 'the solitary monster,' 'the goddess of reptiles,' 'the lord of swine,' 'the evil face,' 'the evil eye,' etc."—*The Signs of the Times*, June 24, 1940.

"To Sol Deus invictus—the sun, *the unconquerable god*—were attributed the world-wide conquests of the Roman power. The greatest and most magnificent temple that ever was built on earth, except only that built by Solomon, was erected by Antonius Pius, emperor of Rome, at Baalbek, in honour of the visible shining sun." *The Two Republics,* p. 197.

"Sun-worship, however, became increasingly popular at Rome in the second and third centuries A.D. The sun-god of Emesa in Syria—*Deus Sol invictus Elagabalus*—was exalted above the older gods of Rome by the Emperor (Macrinus, A.D. 217, taking the name Elagabalus) who, as his priest was identified with the object of his worship... was made the chief worship of the state by Aurelian." *Companion to Roman History,* H. Stuart Jones, p. 302.

"It was openly asserted that the worship of the sun, under his name of Elagabalus, was to supersede all other worship." *The History of Christianity,* H. H. Milman, D.D., vol. 2, p. 175.

"In 274 Aurelian was inspired with the same idea, when he created a new cult of the '*Invincible Sun.*'... In establishing this new State cult, Aurelian in reality proclaimed the dethronement of the old Roman idolatry and the accession of Semitic sun-worship." *Astrology and Religion,* pp. 94-99.

"The ecclesiastical writers... contrasted the 'Sun of Justice' with the '*invincible sun,*' and consented to see in the dazzling orb which illuminated man a symbol of Christ, 'the light of the world.'" *Mysteries of Mithra,* by Franz Cumont, Ph.D., LL.D., p. 193.

"The devotees of Mithra held Sunday sacred because Mithra was identified with the '*invincible sun.*'" W. de.c. Ravenel, of the Smithsonian Institute, quoted in *Sunday,* p. 3.

THE SUN A SYMBOL OF "THE SUN OF RIGHT-EOUSNESS" — NOT A LITERAL OBJECT OF WORSHIP

Nature, rightly understood, speaks to us of the Creator. God intended that natural objects would serve to turn our minds constantly to Him. Thus, the sun in all its glory and power, would remind us of the glory and power of God. Since the inception of sin, the Lord has used the things of nature as visible objects from which spiritual lessons could be drawn. The sun—the "day star" of our planet, "the Light of the world"—is employed in Scripture as the *symbol,* in our *spiritual* experience, of Jesus, the "Day Star," "the Light of the world." See John 9:5; 1:5, 9; 3:19; 8:12; 12:35, 46; Mal. 4:2; Luke 1:78, margin; Eph. 5:14; 2 Pet. 1:19; Rev. 2:28; 22:16; etc.

In my examination, in another outline, of Rev. 7:2; 16:12, I wrote:—"All through Scripture Christ is said to be the "Day-spring," or "Sun-rising." Japan is never once even referred to, much less given such a title, in Scripture. Christ claimed to be 'the Light of the world.' So does Japan! Expositors of Holy Writ, in interpreting the Scriptures, should not heed Japan's blasphemous claim. Jesus Christ is the 'Sunrising,' 'the Light of the world,' 'The Sun of Righteousness'—and the world's only Saviour."

"Satan" means "Adversary," and in his "war" against God his policy is to be shrewd. He employs all the consummate cunning of which his gigantic intellect is capable. The Bible warns us against "the wiles of the devil." "There is nothing that the great deceiver fears so much as that we shall become acquainted with his devices." GC 516. The Revelator describes him as "that old serpent, called the Devil, and Satan, which deceiveth the whole world." Rev. 12:9.

SATAN SEEKS THE PLACE OF GOD

Satan desires to take God's place in our worship and service, so that when rendering homage we shall actually be heeding Satan's will. This he does by substituting his will for God's will—by taking *the things of God*, and, with great subtlety, using *them* in his own service. That is, *using the same things, but for a different purpose.* Thus, the Babylonians (who were controlled by the invincible Lucifer, the real King of Babylon, Isa. 14:4, 12), took the vessels, which had been employed in the service of God in the temple at Jerusalem, and with *them* praised their own gods—even Satan, and his evil minions. See Dan. 5:3-6.

And so it is with all the things of God—Satan's most effective means of deception is to so use them to his own purpose, that people, because of the resemblance to the true things of God, feel that, in employing them in worship, they render homage to their Creator. But, by not heeding the repeated warnings and injunction of the Bible, they are deceived into doing Satan's will, instead of God's.

In many ways this is seen, but particularly in regard to the 4th Commandment of the Decalogue is Satan's subtlety manifested. God's command to "Remember" to keep holy the 7th day as God's Sabbath is explicit enough, yet, despite that, Satan has succeeded in turning the majority of professing Christians away from God's original Command. This is done on the pretext that, because Christ rose on Sun-day, the 1st day of the week, God's law became obsolete, because it was supposed to have been nailed to the cross with the ceremonial law in which types and shadows pointed forward to the death of Jesus, our ever-blessed Lord. There is nothing but Satanic sophistry in this contention. Such a view is positively unscriptural. Many able writers have proved this beyond question.

CAN WE HONOUR CHRIST WHILE DISHONOURING GOD?

How deluded people are when Satan can persuade them to disobey a definite Commandment of the Creator, thus dishonouring God, under the pretext of honouring Christ's resurrection by keeping the Sabbath on the 1st day of the week—that day anciently dedicated to sun worship!!! In this we see Satan's policy in deceiving *"the whole world"* (Rev. 12:9), namely, by using God's Sabbath Commandment for his purpose of deception.

This world, since listening to Satan's insinuations, has absorbed worldly ways, and is bewitched by material things—the things of time and sense. But it is the *invisible* things which are eternal. 2 Cor. 4:18. Thus, the Sabbath-holy *time*, which *cannot be seen or felt*—lifts our hearts and minds beyond mundane things, and it is this *spiritual* institution that God's enemy has chosen as a battle-ground for his wiliest deception. It enables his selfish will to be done, while people think they exalt Christ. All honest hearts will be saved. Many millions of God-fearing Christians have observed the 1st day of the week as the Sabbath, not knowing Satan's machinations, and God has accepted their sincerity. But, in these closing days, when Satan's kingdom is to end, God designs that His people will become acquainted with the part that Sun-day has played in the past, and is destined to play in the terrific struggle which will bring earthly history to its close—"the battle of that great day of God Almighty," Armageddon.

However, thousands of God-fearing Christians each year are now accepting the light, and are yielding obedience to God's Sabbath Commandment, and by preparing for "the last great conflict," are being strengthened "to stand in *the battle in the day of the Lord*." Ezek. 13:5.

Satan will desperately contest for the supremacy. Prophecy makes it very clear that the closing scenes of the controversy between Christ and Satan will be a most terrific struggle over God's Sabbath Commandment, and Satan's counterfeit day, Sun-day.

All honest hearts will heed God's message to come out of Babylon—the religious world, which takes the things of Christ, and uses them for a purpose other than that commanded by God. Rev. 18:4, etc.

CAIN A TYPE

As Cain murdered his brother because Abel refused to follow Satan's altered way of worshipping God, so modern Babylon will demand all the faithful Abels (who stand strictly by God's Commandments) to worship God according to the will of Satan. Cain was selfish to have murdered his brother. It will be selfishness which will order the death-decree upon God's Commandment-keeping people; but, in accordance with Satan's subtlety, *it will be represented under the guise of a benefit to mankind.* The Jews slew Jesus Christ to save their nation. John 11:48-51; 18:14; GC 27. The same argument will be employed again. GC 590, 614, 615.

THE FIRST MURDER AND THE FIRST RECORDED CONFLICT AT MEGIDDO

In a previous pamphlet the importance of the *"first"* and the *"last"* mention was shown. The first use of a thing in the Scripture points to the last. The first occasion usually was something of a *local* nature; the last is that which *involves the world.* Thus, Cain's murder—the *first* recorded in the Scripture—of his brother, because Abel did not worship God in the way he did, foreshadows the final attempt to be made by the world-wide Cain—the Babylonian system—which will seek to destroy the world-wide Abel—the church which keeps the Commandments of God. Rev. 12:17; 14:12.

According to the same principle of the first pointing to the last, the first conflict at *Megiddo*—involving *Israel* and devil-led, *sun-worshipping* Canaanites (see Judg. 4, 5), foreshadows the *last* Megiddo conflict—that world-wide Armageddon, in which Sun-day enforcers, who have been led by "the spirits of devils" (Rev. 16:13, 14), have been contesting with spiritual Israel over Israel's sign (the Sabbath, see Exod. 31:12-17, etc.) of allegiance to God. As in the first conflict, "there was *not* a man left" (Judg. 4:16), so in Armageddon, "the battle of that great day of God Almighty," all Israel's enemies will be destroyed—not one will be left.

Selfishness and self-will are Satanic principles which, when permitted to grow to maturity, produce murder. Those who will persist in doing Satan's will, by continued observance of the false Sabbath (despite God's warning message, which will soon be proclaimed with a mighty voice throughout the world, Rev. 18:1; etc.), will eventually manifest the Satanic traits of character, and like Cain, will endeavour to destroy those who will not follow their way of worship. Then God will no longer tolerate the insults to His majesty, nor permit Satan to destroy His people. Instead of the threatening hosts, deceived by Satan, slaughtering God's faithful ones, they themselves are slain in "the great battle of God Almighty"—Armageddon. Rev. 16:12-16.

As he does with other things of God, *Satan uses the prophecies, which predict this coming world-wide Armageddon*, to deceive the people. The *same* prophecies that God gave to show His people the dangers which await *them* Satan gives another interpretation, and Futurists, and others, are led to believe that "Armageddon" is a literal military "war" to be fought in Palestine. Here God's enemy still takes the *things* of God and, using them for a different purpose, deceives the people.

As I have dealt with these themes more fully in other places I shall not repeat myself here. We have shown that *Satan uses the things of God* in order to lead the world into his ways. The Bible is replete with the revelation of this fact. And so it is with the east, the place of sunrise.

THE SUN A SYMBOL OF CHRIST

The sun is the Bible *symbol* of Christ. The rising sun *symbolizes* the scattering of our dark night of sin with the "healing" rays of "the Sun of Righteousness." Mal. 4:2. While it is our privilege to see in the sunrise a *symbol* of Christ, we are forbidden to worship anything, or anyone other than God. Exod. 20:3-6; Acts 14:11-15; Rev. 22:8, 9. Satan inculcated into the human race the worship of the sun. "Who *changed* the truth of God into a lie, and worshipped and served the creature rather than the Creator." Rom. 1:25. Thus, idolatry is using something of God's in a way not ordained of God—and in a way that degrades God in the human mind; takes away God's glory, and renders one a subject of God's enemy. It will be noted in this, and many other instances, that Satan's deception lies in making *literal* what God has set out as a *symbol*. In the Lord's

Supper the same feature is observed. When Christ said, "This is My body," He obviously intended that the bread was to be employed as a *symbol*. Gigantic errors have come about through interpreting this *literally* instead of *symbolically*. In Rev. 12 God gave a *symbol* of Satan. A *literal* interpretation of this red dragon led to the belief that Satan is a grotesque monster. If space permitted, it could be pointed out that the foundational errors of the Papacy (and most last-day errors) have come into being by taking a *literal* instead of a *spiritual* interpretation of certain statements and prophecies of the Bible. And this literal interpretation has resulted in a species of idolatry.

LITERAL OR SYMBOLICAL?

In the days of the old economy the Sanctuary was built to face the East. Then, the *literal* East did enter into matters relating to God's worship. Those who worshipped God turned toward the manifestation of God in the Most Holy Place. When Israel apostatized Ezekiel saw the priests *"with their backs toward* the temple of the Lord, and their *faces toward the east*; and they worshipped the *sun toward the east."* Ezek. 8:16.

In Ezek. 43:1-4 we read:—"Afterward he brought me to the gate, even the gate that looketh *toward the east*: and behold, the glory of the God of Israel came *from the way of the east*... and the earth shined with His glory.... And the glory of the Lord *came into* the house by the way of the gate whose prospect is *toward the east."*

In Ezek. 10:19; 11:1, 22, 23, the glory of the Lord is said to have departed from the Lord's house by the way of the east gate. Israel's sins had caused God to withdraw His presence from the temple. However, God did not leave His people without hope, and so He encouraged them with the thought that He would return. The promises concerning the magnificent temple brought to view in Ezek. 40-48 were provisional, and it is generally recognized that the proper interpretation of those chapters is in connection with the Christian church. This is the interpretation given in the Spirit of Prophecy, as we have noted elsewhere. The river of life which emerges "from under the threshold of the house *eastward*: for the forefront of the house stood *toward the east"* (Ezek. 47:1-3) is applied by the Spirit of Prophecy to the work of the church. AA 13-16; 7T 24; 9T 96. Thus, the east of this temple (which applies in this dispensation of the spiritual application of the things of

Israel) is a *spiritual*, and not primarily a literal east. "The glory of the God of Israel" which made *"the earth"* shine *"with His glory"* (Ezek. 43:2) is applied spiritually in Rev. 18:1, for there we read: *"and the earth was lightened with His glory."* This, of course, is the loud cry of the Third Angel's Message. The message in Rev. 7:1-3, is pictured as having come from the east—*the place of sun-rising*. All of this, *primarily*, refers to a spiritual east—as is presented in the prophetic picture of the church under the emblem of a temple on the mountain of Israel, where God's glory is pictured as coming into the temple by way of the *east* gate.

The fact that in Mal. 4:2 we read: "But unto you that fear my name shall the *Sun of righteousness arise* with healing in his wings," shows that a *spiritual* application was made in Old Testament times of the *sun rising in the East*. As the literal sun arose in the east and scattered the darkness, so Jesus arises and shines upon our *spiritual* darkness, and gives us light. 2 Pet. 1:19. As Satan uses the things of Christ to deceive the people, he caused them to worship the *literal* sun in the *literal* east. Not content with the sun and the east as *symbols*, the people became idolatrous and worshipped the sun while paying due respect to the east.

Mosheim says:—"Nearly all the people of the East, before the Christian era, were accustomed to *worship with their faces directed toward the sun rising*." Then he proceeds to state that Christians in the early church "retained" this custom.

"How extensive and comprehensive the Christian worship toward the east was, Dr. Dodgson shows in a note to Tertullian's Apology, chapter 16:—

'Christians *prayed to the east,* as the type of Christ the Sun of Righteousness, whence also in *baptism* they turned to the east to confess Christ, and *their churches* were towards the east.'" *History of the Sabbath*, p. 320.

In the chapter on "Why Christ Rose on Sunday?" other extracts are given showing the popularity of this custom. Sun-day keeping more easily obtained an entrance into the Christian church because the sun and the east were regarded in a *literal* sense, instead of God's *symbol* of light and truth.

By this *literal* application Satan succeeded in deceiving so many into the idolatry of sun-worship. In the kindliest way possible, I wish to state that the interpretation of prophecy regarding the *literal* gathering of nations to Palestine for "Armageddon"—a part of Futurism—is based upon the same erroneous *principle* of applying *literally* what should be applied *spiritually*—though some very godly men have taught it, and still believe in it.

The *literal* teachings of Futurism (regarding Israel and Palestine) Satan devised as a system of prophetic interpretation opposed to the Third Angel's Message—the truth that makes people free from Satan's deceptions concerning the mark of the beast (the *spiritual* mark of rebellion against the will of God) and frees them from darkness and bondage.

Satan is, by no means, Omnipotent—that is a fact for which every believer in Christ as King and Lord of all, is profoundly thankful. In Luke 11:21-23 Christ illustrates the power of two mighty ones—Himself and Satan. And blessed be God and His Beloved Son, our Lord and Master is the stronger.

OUR DEPENDENCE UPON JESUS

In nature, all life is absolutely dependent upon the sun for existence. And so, all spiritual life depends entirely upon Jesus, "the Sun of Righteousness," "the Light of the world." As the sun is the mighty monarch of natural things, so Jesus is the Almighty Monarch of all creation—and the supreme Lord in the spiritual realms. The sun is the *symbol* of the invincible Lord, for "He hath triumphed gloriously" over His enemies. At the time of the Exodus He overthrew the sun-worshipping Egyptians, who endeavoured to compel Israel to disobey God by breaking the Sabbath Commandment. See Ex. 5:5-19.

The Israelites were encouraged by the words: "The Lord shall *fight* for you." Ex. 14:14. "And the *Lord* overthrew the Egyptians in the midst of the sea.... Thus the Lord saved Israel." vs. 27, 30. "Then sang Moses and the children of Israel this song.... He hath triumphed gloriously... the *Lord* is a *man of war*... Thy right hand, O Lord, is become glorious in power: Thy right hand, O Lord, hath dashed in pieces the enemy." Ex. 15:1-6. These experiences of *national* Israel are typical (1 Cor. 10:6, margin; 11, margin; Rom. 15:4) of what will occur in the experiences of *spiritual* Israel before their final and complete departure from this world—spiritual Egypt. Rev. 11:8.

THE DESTRUCTION OF PERSECUTING POWERS

The pursuing, persecuting powers of Egypt were all destroyed by the God of Israel. We read:—"There remained not so much as *one of them*." Ex. 14:28. In this is prefigured the complete overthrow of all those in the last days who will seek to destroy Israel. Isa. 51:9-23 points back to Israel's experience in coming out of Rahab (an old name for Egypt, see Ps. 89:10, margin), when "the dragon" (Rev. 12:7-9) "was wounded." Reference is made to the dividing of the Red Sea:—"Art thou not it which hath dried the sea, the waters of the great deep, that hath made the depth of the sea a way for the ransomed to pass over?" Isa. 51:10. Quoting from this chapter, God's servant says:—"The eye of God, looking down the ages, was fixed upon the crisis which His people are to meet, when earthly powers shall be arrayed against them. Like the captive exile, they will be in fear of death by starvation or by violence. But the *Holy One who divided the Red Sea before Israel*, will manifest His mighty power and turn their captivity." GC 634. Thus, the Spirit of God points out the typical nature of this experience.

As in the *first* great battle fought by "the waters of *Megiddo*" (Judg. 5:19) Israel triumphed over the devil-led sun-worshipping Canaanites, when "there was *not a man left*" (Judg. 4:16), so in the destruction of the hosts of Pharaoh at the Red Sea, "There remained *not* so much as *one of them*." One of the most definite laws of prophetic interpretation is, that what was *local* and *national* in the days of *literal* Israel, is *typical of world-wide events* in the last days—in which the *church* will be involved. Thus, in these typical victories of national Israel over her foes, we see the world-wide destruction which will surely come to spiritual *Israel's enemies* in that *symbolical* place "called in the *Hebrew* tongue Armageddon,"—that anti-typical *Megiddo* conflict, which is to be *world-wide* in its scope.

The contest, then, as in Egypt, or at Megiddo, will be loyalty to God by abiding by his complete will—or following the deceptions of Satan. It will be either the seal, sign of God, or the mark of the beast—the 7th day Sabbath, the sign of God's kingdom or the 1st day, Sun-day, the mark of Satan's kingdom.

As in the typical Megiddo conflict, in Armageddon—the *anti-typical, world-wide battle*—Satan will seek to destroy "the

Israel of God;" but instead, the tables will be turned, for there will not be "a man left" when "the unconquered Son" of God (*symbolized* by "the unconquered Sun"), delivers His people from the fury of their foes. He is "the *invincible* Son," and all who trust in Him will triumph with Him in "the battle of that great day of God Almighty." Notice these words of God's servant:—"*The battle of Armageddon* is soon to be fought. He on whose vesture is written the name, *King of kings, and Lord of lords*, is soon to lead forth the armies of heaven." 6T 406. The title "King of kings, and Lord of lords" is found three times in the New Testament. It is in the battle of Armageddon that Jesus proves that He is "King of kings." See 1 Tim. 6:15; Rev. 17:14; 19:16.

"Who is this King of Glory? The Lord strong and mighty, the Lord *mighty in battle*." Ps. 24:8. This, His adversaries will discover, when He comes to "judge and make *war*" (Rev. 19:11) upon Satan, "the defeated Sun-god"—the author of Sun-day observance—in "*the battle* (or "*war*") of that great day of God Almighty." Rev. 16:14.

Let us thank God for "His unspeakable gift" (2 Cor. 9:15)—"*the invincible* Lord," "the unconquered Son."

CHAPTER **VII**

Sunday–The Weekly Day of the Sun

In order for us to give a full answer as to why Christ rose the first day of the week we must consider how important Sunday was in the calendar of sun-worship. The 25th of December was the day of *Natalis Solis Invicti*, that is, the birth of the invincible sun. This was the *yearly* festival. But its annual visitation could not be regarded as the most powerful in influencing the minds of mankind. Something with more frequency would be needful to accomplish the work of imprinting indelibly upon the human race the designs of the devil in leading men away from God's perfect plan. To accomplish the nefarious devices of Satan, Sunday was made the *weekly* festival of the sun god. "The sanctification of Sunday" was one of the principle doctrines of the sun worshippers.—*Encyclopedia Britannica,* Art. "Mithras," 11th Ed., of 1911, p. 624.

David Jennings, D.D., born 1691, an able writer of antiquities, said of *Sunday*:—"The day which the heathen consecrated in general to the worship and honour of their chief god, the sun, which, *according to our computation*, was the final day of the week." *Jewish Antiquities*, book 3, chapter 3.

Verstegan adds his testimony:—"The most ancient Germans being pagan and having appropriated the *first day of the week* to the peculiar *adoration of the sun*, whereof that day doth yet in our English tongue retain the name of Sunday."—*Verstegan's Antiquities*, p. 10, London, 1605, A.D.

The ancient pagans dedicated particular days to different deities, and they regarded Sunday (the 1st day of the week) as "the venerable day of the Sun," or Baal's day, which means "Lord's Day." The 7th day of the week is the Lord's Day. (See Ex. 20:8-11; Isa. 58:13; Mark 2:28; Rev. 1:10.) Sun-day is Baal's day—Satan's counterfeit Sabbath.

"The devotees of Mithra held *Sunday sacred* because Mithra was identified with the 'invincible sun.'"—W. de.c. Ravenel, of the Smithsonian Institute, Washington, D.C., U.S.A., in a letter of November 21, 1923, quoted in *Sunday*, p. 3.

"Sunday, over which the sun presided was especially holy."— Franz Cumont, Ph.D., LL.D., in his *The Mysteries of Mithras,* Chicago, 1910, pp. 190-192.

"Sunday being the day on which the Gentiles solemnly adored that planet, and called it Sunday."—Thomas H. Morer, *Dialogues on the Lord's Day,* p. 32, London.

"A special holy day (or holiday) was Sunday—the sun's day, dedicated by the heathen to the sun.

"The pre-eminence assigned to the dies solis (day of the sun) also certainly contributed to the general recognition of Sunday as a holiday."—*Astrology and Religion,* p. 163.

"Sunday, so called because this day was anciently dedicated to the sun, or to its worship."—*Webster's International Dictionary.*

The North British Review terms it "the wild solar holiday of all pagan times."

THE SABBATH—OR SUNDAY?

We have seen how the pagan times of December 25 and the Easter seasons came into the Christian church. The sun god was certainly flattered when the church, ordained to oppose Satan's customs, introduced them as some of the chief festivals of the church. But they were only annual events and not so important in the scheme of things as a weekly reminder of the power of the "invincible sun." Well might one, in utter amazement, wonder how the church turned aside from the observance of the seventh day, which is so much stressed throughout the Bible as the sign of God's almighty, creative power. Being the only command in the Decalogue prefaced with "Remember," it surely is an indication of the importance of the Sabbath command in the mind of the Almighty Creator and Lawgiver. God's Omniscience is also thus revealed, for it shows that He knew that this would be the one command particularly selected for attack by the enemy. He knew that the proud angel who contested with Him in glory would contest with Him upon the earth *over the issue of Lordship*. The Sabbath is the sign of God's almighty and invincible power—the insignia of His Godhead. See Gen. 2:1-3; Ex. 20:8-11; Isa. 58:12-14; 66:22, 23; Ezek. 20:12, 20, etc. Contrary to popular ideas, the Sabbath is mentioned fifty-nine times in the New Testament, where it is still regarded as being as intact as when first made at creation. The first day of the week is mentioned only eight times in the New Testament—merely as an ordinary day of the week, without any title whatever. "The Lord's Day" of Rev. 1:10 can be no other than the seventh day, which is the Lord's Day from the dawn of creation. Christ, the Lord and Creator (see John 1:1-3, 14; Col. 1:16; Ephes. 3:9; Heb. 1:1-3, etc.) said that He "*is Lord* also *of the Sabbath*." Mark 2:28. Therefore "The Lord's Day" is the Sabbath of which Christ claimed to be the Lord.

The fact that the sun was called Baal—"Lord"—was because Satan, the author of sun-worship, had deluded mankind to worship him in this false fashion, and had blasphemously put himself in the place of God. There are two Lords pressing for man's undivided devotion—one the Creator, the Lord of glory, the Maker of the Seventh-day Sabbath; and the other, a fallen creature, striving for the lordship of man—the maker of Sunday observance. Both are called "Lord"—who will win the contest? The answer is given in the fact that Jesus Christ rose the first day of the week. But more about that later.

In neither the Old nor the New Testaments do we find any authority for the observance of the first day of the week in the church of Jesus Christ. Neither the apostles nor Jesus Christ Himself ever taught or observed that day. The early Christian believers did not observe it until several centuries after the ascension, when the compromise with pagan sun-worship had been formed. Standing firmly upon authentic historical data, the historian finds that Sunday was never anything but a solar holiday of heathenism until adopted into the church by leading ecclesiastics, some time after the New Testament had been written.

HOW SUNDAY-KEEPING GREW
WITHIN THE CHURCH

How did this change came about from the Sabbath, or seventh day of the week, to Sunday, the first day? Like all other practices and rites from paganism, the change was a gradual one. When the Roman Empire began to profess Jesus Christ, the multitudes were very unwilling to part with their pagan customs and habits; therefore the leaders of the church baptized these new "converts", but allowed them to continue much of the round of pagan practices as they had previously done.

If we have been told that Sunday originated with the apostles in honour of the resurrection of our Lord, let us remove this error from our minds. The recognition of Sunday was common in all lands where sun worship was the religion. This was true for *centuries before Christ was born.*

In the earlier generations the enemy of righteousness had corrupted the truth of God by his counterfeits, and by leading the world to pay respect to Sunday he was preparing for his greatest triumph—namely, to introduce into the Christian church the day which anciently had been dedicated to his worship.

Of course, we need to remember that the ancient worshippers of the sun did not observe it as we do the Sabbath—they did not cease to work on Sun-day. *Dio Cassius,* Book 37, chapter 17, shows that devoting a day to a duty by engaging in no "serious occupations" was as late as 220 A.D. considered an extravagant fashion in Palestine.

Neander, "father of modern church history," says:—

"The festival of Sunday, like other festivals, was always only a human ordinance, and it was far from the intentions of the apostles to establish a divine command in this respect, far from them, and from the early apostolic church, to transfer the laws of the Sabbath to Sunday. Perhaps at the *end of the second century* a false application of this kind had begun to take place; for men appear *by that time to have considered labouring on Sunday as a sin."* Quoted in *History of the Sabbath,* p. 249.

It would take us beyond our objective to give the history of the struggle which went on within the Christian church following the death of the last representatives of the apostles' days—the worldly tendencies of power-craving bishops, and the watering down of the gospel to suit the worldly, carnal natures of the pagan world. The Sabbath continued to be observed for some centuries after Christ, while the Sun-day was pressed into use by apostatizing bishops.

Socrates, a church historian of the fifth century, writing as a personal eyewitness of customs existing in the Christian church in general (A.D. 391), says:—"Almost all churches throughout the world celebrate the *sacred* mysteries [Lord's Supper] on the Sabbath of every week." Then in a footnote is added, "That is upon Saturday."—*Ecclesiastical History,* book 5, chapter 22, p. 289.

From this writer we see that practically the whole Christian church kept Saturday as the Sabbath up to A.D. 391. The bishops of Rome, to suppress the Sabbath by casting a gloom over it, had ordered the churches to fast on Saturday. Pope Sylvester (314-335) thus ordered the churches, and, later, Pope Innocent (402-416) made this "a binding law." "And in this difference it stood a long time together, till in the end the *Roman Church* obtained the cause, and *Saturday* became a fast, almost through all parts of the Western world.... Which I have noted here, in its proper place, that we might know the better how the matter stood between the *Lord's Day*, and the *Sabbath*; how hard a thing it was for the one to get the mastery of the other."—*History of the Sabbath,* book 2, chapter 2, p. 45, London, 1636.

How could the Sabbath have been changed by the apostles, when it was so hard to make this change centuries after their decease? Rev. Joseph Bingham, M.A., writes:—

"The ancient Christians were *very careful in the observation of Saturday,* or the seventh day, which was the ancient Jewish Sabbath. Some observed it as a fast, others as a festival; *but all unanimously agreed in keeping it* as a more solemn day of religious worship and adoration.... Athanasius likewise tells us, that they held *religious assemblies on the Sabbath,* not because they were infected with Judaism, but to worship Jesus, the Lord of the Sabbath. Epiphanius says the same."—*Antiquities of the Christian Church,* vol. VII, chapter 3, section 1, pp. 52-53.

Many other authorities could be quoted.

THE APOSTATE CHURCH INTRODUCES PAGAN RITES AND CEREMONIES

"In the interval between the days of the apostles and the conversion of Constantine, the Christian commonwealth changed its aspect.... Rites and ceremonies, of which neither Paul nor Peter ever heard, crept silently into use, and then claimed the rank of divine institutions."—*Ancient Church,* Preface, pp. XV, XVI, by Dr. W. D. Killen.

"It is not necessary to go into a subject which the diligence of Protestant writers has made familiar to most of us. The use of temples, and these dedicated to particular saints... holy water, asylums, holy days and seasons, use of calendars, processions... *are all of pagan origin*, and sanctified by their adoption into the church."—*Development of Christian Doctrine*, John Henry Cardinal Newman, p. 373. London: Longmans, Greene & Co., 1906.

No wonder that Edward B. Tylor in his book, *Primitive Culture*, says:—"*Our most important ecclesiastical feast* days are but survivals of *ancient solar festivals.*" Cardinal Newman, as shown in the above extract, endeavours to justify their existence in the church.

THE REVIVAL OF SUN-WORSHIP

Shortly after our Blessed Lord rose upon the first day of the week—Sunday—Satan aroused himself and exerted all his might to oppose the church of the Crucified and Risen One. Sun worship, as if resurrected into new life, swept the world with renewed vigour. This renewed sun worship was known as "Mithraism." This new form of heathen worship soon captured the Caesars, invaded the Roman armies and the centers of learning, and was embraced by the higher classes of society. Satan knew that to oppose the dignity of the Christian teachings he had to present a philosophy which was more fascinating than the more crude form of paganism. He would have to make a pretense of holding up high standards of morality, while introducing into the church the day which was dedicated anciently to his honour. Alexandria and Rome soon became important Mithran centers, and, in fact, history records that in "the middle of the third century Mithraism seemed on the verge of becoming the universal religion," and that it "*became the greatest antagonist of Christianity.*" Some of the peculiar doctrines enunciated by its priests were "the immortality of the soul," "the use of bell and candle, holy water and communion, sanctification of Sunday, and the 25th of December."—*Encyclopedia Britannica*, art. "Mithra," 11th edition.

Sun worship became the national religion. Soon it enjoyed imperial protection, and this, of course, assisted its world-wide spread. Elagabalus was one of the first of these emperors. The name he bore was the Phoenician name of the black conical stone that had been found in Emesa, in Syria, and which was said to have fallen from the sky, and was a picture of the sun.

"If we may believe the biographies in the Augustine history, a more ambitious scheme of a *universal religion* had dawned upon the mind of the emperor [Elagabalus (201-222), son of the senator Various Marcellus]. The Jewish, the Samaritan, even the Christian, were to be fused and recast *into one great system*, of which *the sun was to be the central object* of adoration.

"It was openly asserted that the worship of the sun, under the name of Elagabalus, was to supersede all other worship."—*The History of Christianity*, Dean Henry Hart Milman, book 2, chapter 8, par. 20 and 22.

Thus, through Elagabalus, Satan endeavoured to become the Lord over all. This religious, despotical emperor died a terrible death.

Some fifty years after that attempt to erect sun-worship in the Roman Empire, the Emperor Aurelian once more fostered its interest. Not contented with the restoration of the temple of the sun in the midst of the ruins of Palmyra, this renowned emperor built a magnificent temple of the sun at Rome.

Later emperors continued this sun-worship. Constantine caused the minting of many coins with figures or busts of the sun god, putting above or below it such words as "To the unconquered sun."

"The devotion of Constantine was more peculiarly directed to the genius of the sun.... The sun was *universally* celebrated as the *invincible* guide and protector of Constantine."—*Decline and Fall of the Roman Empire*, by Gibbon.

Constantine's devotion to the sun led him, in A. D. 321, to endeavour to cause all to observe the day dedicated to its worship. He made the sun's day a legal holiday by declaring, "Let all the judges and townspeople and the occupation of all trades rest on the *venerable day of the sun*."—Edict of March 7, 321.

In the *Encyclopedia Britannica*, ninth edition, article *"Sunday,"* this law of Constantine's is declared to be "the earliest recognition of the observance of Sunday as a *legal duty*." It is "unquestionably the first law, either ecclesiastical or civil, by which the Sabbatical observance of that day is known to have been ordained." *Clark's Encyclopedia*, article *"Sabbath."*

Speaking of Constantine the *Encyclopedia Britannica* says:—

"He was at best only half heathen, half Christian, who could seek to combine the worship of Christ with the worship of Apollo, having the name of one and the figure of the other impressed upon his coins, and ordering the *observance of Sunday* under the name dies solis (day of the sun)."—Quoted in *Fathers of the Catholic Church*, p. 323.

"Mithra's holy day was Sunday. On that day work was forbidden to his worshippers… the law of Constantine… was an attempt on the part of the emperor to combine the practices of Mithraism, which had been his faith, and those of Christianity, to which he had been converted." — *The Story of Superstition*, p. 180.

Edwards, in his work, *Sunday in History*, page 93, says:—

"It will be remembered that this law [the Sunday edict] of 321 was made at least two years before Constantine professed to be converted to Christianity; that he was at that time a full-fledged sun-worshipping heathen." "When he professed to become a Christian, in order to carry his sun-worshipping pagans with him, he simply called 'the venerable *day of the sun*,' the day of the Son of God; but left the spelling of the word as though it were the day of the *Sun* of the *Sun God*. By this time many of the leaders, officers in the professed church of Christ, were half-converted heathen, Constantine with the rest; and some of them were still sun-worshippers. It is easy to see how Constantine being then in the church and also emperor, and, to quite a degree leader of both church and state, could, through the Sunday move, unite the sun-worshipping pagans with the Sunday Christians; and thus he did."

Concerning Constantine's action with regard to Sunday observance Dean Stanley remarks:—

"The retention of the old pagan name 'Dies Solis,' or 'Sunday,' for the weekly pagan festival, is, in great measure, owing to the union of pagan and Christian sentiment with which the first day of the week was recommended by Constantine to his subjects, pagan and Christian alike, as the 'venerable *day of the sun*.'… It was his mode of harmonizing discordant religions of the empire under one common institution." — *Lectures on the History of the Eastern Church*, p. 184.

As to whether Constantine was seeking to enforce a heathen or a Christian festival, Professor Webster makes the following pertinent statement:—

"This legislation by Constantine probably bore no relation to Christianity; it appears, on the contrary, that the emperor, in his capacity of Pontifex Maximus, was only adding the *day of the sun*, the worship of which was then firmly established in the Roman

Empire, to the other ferial days of the sacred calendar."—*Rest Days*, Prof. H. Webster, Ph.D. (University of Nebraska), p. 122.

So willing were church leaders to adopt heathen festivals that even heathen authors reproached them for it. Faustus, a pagan of the fourth century, in speaking to the Christians, declared:—

"You celebrate the solemn festivities of the *Gentiles*… and as to their manners, those you have retained without any alteration. Nothing distinguishes you from the pagans except that you hold your assemblies apart from them."—Faustus (a non-Christian) to St. Augustine; cited in *History of the Intellectual Development of Europe,* John W. Draper, M.D., LL.D., vol. 1, p. 310.

Tertullian, early in the third century, frankly admitted:—

"Others, with greater regard to good manners, it must be confessed, suppose that the *sun is the god of the Christians*, because it *is a well-known fact that we pray toward the east*, or because *we make Sunday a day of festivity*. What then? Do you do less than this?… It is you at all events, who have admitted the sun into the calendar of the week; and you have selected its day, in preference to the preceding day.... You who reproach us with *sun and Sunday* should consider your proximity to us." — *Ad Nations,* book 1, chapter 13.

Tertullian had no other excuse for their Sunday keeping than that they did not do any worse than the heathen. Not only did the church adopt the heathen festivals, but Gregory Thaumaturgus allowed the converts to celebrate them in the same degrading manner as the heathen.

"When Gregory perceived that the ignorant multitude persisted in their idolatry, on account of the pleasures and sensual gratifications which they enjoyed at the pagan festivals, he granted them a permission to indulge themselves in like pleasures, hoping that, in the process of time, they would return of their own accord, to a more virtuous and regular course of life."—*Ecclesiastical History,* by J. L. Mosheim, D.D., in vol. 2, book 1, chapter 4, paragraph 3, footnote.

With leaders and congregations of that kind one could hardly expect them to retain the "Sabbath of the Lord," or any other gospel truth in its purity.

"On the other hand, the ecclesiastic writers… contrasted the 'Sun of justice' with the 'invincible sun,' and consented to see it, the dazzling orb which illuminated man a symbol of Christ, 'the light of the world.' Should we be astonished if the multitudes of devotees failed always to observe the subtle distinctions of the doctors, and if in obedience to a pagan custom they rendered to the radiant star of the day the homage which orthodoxy reserved for God? In the *fifth century, not only heretics, but even faithful followers were still wont to bow their heads toward its dazzling disc as it rose above the horizon,* and to murmur the prayer, 'Have mercy on us.'"—*Mysteries of Mithra*," p. 193, by Franz Cumont, Ph.D., LL.D.

Rev. William Federick declares:—

"The Gentiles were an idolatrous people who *worshipped the sun,* and *Sunday was their most sacred day.* Now, in order to reach the people in this new field, it seems but natural, as well as necessary, to make Sunday the rest day of the church.... At this time it became necessary for the church to either adopt the Gentiles' day or else have the Gentiles change their day. To change the Gentiles' day would have been an offence and a stumbling block to them. The church could naturally reach them better by keeping their day.... There was no need in causing an unnecessary offence by dishonouring their day."—*Three Prophetic Days, or Sunday the Christians' Sabbath,* pp. 169, 170.

Here is a frank admission from a Sunday keeper that respect for Sunday originated with sun-worshipping Gentiles. With such specious and worldly reasoning no wonder the god of sun-worship wears a sardonic smile!

Morer, an English Churchman, says:—

"The Christians thought fit to keep the same day and the same name of it, that they might not appear causelessly peevish, and by that means hinder the conversion of the Gentiles, and bring a greater prejudice than might otherwise be taken against the gospel." —*Dialogues on the Lord's Day,* p. 23.

We shall now hear from the Roman Catholic Church why they adopted the pagan Sunday:—

"The church took the pagan philosophy and made it the buckler of faith against the heathen. She took the pagan Roman pantheon, temple of all the gods, and made it sacred to all the martyrs; so it stands to this day. *She took the pagan Sunday and made it the Christian Sunday.* She took *the pagan Easter* and made it the feast we celebrate during this season....

"The sun was a foremost god with heathendom.... There is, in truth, something royal, kingly about the sun, making it a fit emblem of Jesus, the Sun of justice. Hence the church in these countries would seem to have said, 'Keep that old pagan name. It shall remain consecrated, sanctified.' And thus the *pagan Sunday,* dedicated to balder [the god of light and peace], became the Christian Sunday, sacred to Jesus."—*The Catholic World,* vol. 58, no. 348, March, 1894, p. 809.

Referring to the establishment of Sunday as the Sabbath, the *North British Review*, vol. 18, page 409, says:—"That very day was the Sunday of their heathen neighbours and respective countrymen; and patriotism gladly united with expediency in making it at once their Lord's day and their Sabbath."

Professor H. Webster calls Sunday a pagan institution which was engrafted on to Christianity:—

"The early Christians had at first adopted the Jewish seven-day week, with its numbered week days, but by the close of the third century A.D. this began to give way to the planetary week; and in the fourth and fifth centuries the pagan designations became generally accepted in the western half of Christendom. The use of the planetary names by Christians attests the growing influence of astrological speculations introduced by converts from paganism.... During these same centuries the spread of Oriental solar worship, especially that of 'Mithra,' in the Roman world, had already led to the substitution by pagans of dies Solis for dies Saturni, as the first day of the planetary week.... *Thus gradually a pagan institution was ingrafted on Christianity."*—Rest Days*, Prof. H. Webster, pp. 220, 221.

"Sunday (dies solis… 'day of the sun,' because dedicated to the sun), the first day of the week, was adopted by the early Christians as a day of worship. The 'sun' of Latin adoration they interpreted as the 'Sun of Righteousness.'... No regulations for its observance are laid down in the New Testament, nor, indeed, is its observance even enjoined."—*Schaff-Herzog Encyclopedia of Religious Knowledge,* vol. IV, art. "Sunday," P. 2259.

"The first day of the week, named after the sun, and therefore an evident relic of sun worship. In French it is *Dimanche*, in Italian *Dominica*, both from Dominus, 'The Lord.' Christians, with the exception of the Seventh-day Adventists, have substituted it as a day of rest and prayer in lieu of the Jewish Sabbath."—*Curiosities of Popular Customs*, Wm. S. Walsh, art. "Sunday," p. 901.

Seventh-day Adventists refuse to keep the Sun-day because, in doing so, they would dishonour God, and our Lord and Saviour Jesus Christ. There is a "Lord" behind the sun—that "Lord" is the self-willed Lucifer, the proud, fallen angel, who contested for supremacy against the Lord of Creation. Because they love their Creator, Adventists refuse to follow the hypnotic sway of "the prince of this world," but, rather, stand with the crucified Jesus—the despised and rejected of men—and worship God with their back turned toward the east; away from the "invincible sun."

The Sunday School Advocate endeavours to trace the origin of Sunday in the time of sun-worshippers:—

"In the days of very long ago the people of the world began to give names to everything and turned sounds of the lips into words, so that the words could speak a thought. In those days the people worshipped the sun because it was kind and gave to them heat and light. By and by after many words were made to tell them of many thoughts about many things the people became Christians and were ruled by an emperor whose name was Constantine. This emperor made Sunday the Christian Sabbath, because of the blessing of light and heat which came from the sun. So our *Sunday is a sun-day*, isn't it?"—Issue of December 31, 1921.

In a book published by Richard T. Smith, M.D., of London, and issued with the approval of the Lord's Day Committee of the Wesleyan Methodist Church, an unusually frank statement is made in reference to the real origin of the Sunday Sabbath. Concerning the name of the day the author says:—

"It is very interesting to note the three names that are given to this seventh [first] day to distinguish it from the other six. 1. The name "Sunday" links us with our ancestors, and we cannot but admire and feel a fellow touch with them as they recognized and *worshipped the sun* as the source of their happiness; 'the great orb of day' flooding the world with light and heat and beauty. No earnest Christian would ever sympathise with the iconoclast who wanted to erase that word.... Certainly science will not lightly part with the *sun-day.*"

This statement, and the one that follows, give Satan pleasure and Christ pain. On page 25 the author says:—

"Now we do not find any account in the New Testament of the Lord's Day being substituted for the Sabbath [seventh day] by command; it seems to have originated as an instinct [from Satan], or as a gracious, thankful recognition of the glory and happiness of the day on which the Saviour of the world had risen again from the dead, thereby proving His triumph over sin and death."—Quoted in *The Signs of the Times*, July 7, 1919.

However, in these last days, those who will best honour Christ's resurrection will turn from the observance of Sunday, which was instituted by Christ's enemy. Many thousands of people who now are observing Sunday in honour of Christ, will yet honour Him by keeping the 7th day Sabbath.

We bring this chapter to a conclusion giving Dr. Hiscox's solemn question and declaration:—

"There was and is a commandment to keep holy the Sabbath day, but that Sabbath was not Sunday. It will be said, however, and with some show of triumph, that the Sabbath was transferred from the seventh to the first day of the week, with all its duties, privileges and sanctions. Earnestly desiring information on this subject, which I have studied for many years, I ask, 'Where can the record of such a transaction be found?' Not in the New Testament, absolutely not. There is no Scriptural evidence of the change of the Sabbath institution from the seventh to the first day of the week.

"I wish to say that this Sabbath question, in this aspect of it, is the gravest and most perplexing question connected with Christian institutions which at present claims attention from Christian people; and the only reason that it is not a more disturbing element in Christian thought and in religious discussions, is because the Christian world has settled down content on the conviction that somehow a transference has taken place at the beginning of Christian history....

"To me it seems unaccountable that Jesus, during three years' intercourse with His disciples, often conversing with them upon the Sabbath question, discussing it in some of its various aspects, freeing it from its false glosses, never alluded to any transference of the day; also, that during forty days of His resurrection life, no such thing was intimated. Nor, so far as we know, did the Spirit, which was given to bring to their remembrance all things whatsoever that He said unto them, deal with this question. Nor yet did the inspired apostles, in preaching the gospel, founding churches, counseling and instructing those founded, discuss or approach the subject.

"Of course, I quite well know that Sunday did come into use in early Christian history as a religious day, as we learn from the Christian Fathers and other sources. But *what a pity* that it comes branded *with the mark of paganism*, and christened *with the name of the sun god*, when adopted and sanctioned by the papal apostasy, and bequeathed as a sacred legacy to Protestantism!"—Dr. Edward T. Hiscox, author of *The Baptist Manual*, in a paper read before a New York Ministers' Conference, held November 13, 1893.

Yes, indeed, what a pity!

CHAPTER **VIII**

Sun-day and Babylon
of the Apocalypse

*S*un-day was the most important day in ancient Babylon's religious services, as it is the most sacred day of spiritual Babylon. The following quotation is from the pen of Murl Vance:—

"When we go to the encyclopedia to find out who named the days of the week as we have them to-day, we find that, just as we expected, the ancient *Babylonians named this day, and dedicated it to the sun*… the sun was only a symbol, the real being who was worshipped being Lucifer himself. When we find the sun-god pictured with horns, hoofs, a tail, and a pitchfork, being addressed in worship as 'the evil one,' 'the destroyer,' and 'the great dragon,' we need have no doubt as to who it is that is being worshipped.

"Other historians also add their support as to the source of the day of the sun. Salomon Reinach, the French historian, declares in his 'Orpheus, a History of Religions,' English translation, page 39: 'In their calendar, the Babylonians distinguish between propitious and unpropitious, working and non-working days. Among the latter, it is believed, were the *first days of every septet*, to the number of four per lunar month. This constituted the Babylonian Shabbatum, analogous to the Biblical Sabbath.'

"The Century Dictionary and Encyclopedia declares, under the article 'Sunday': 'The name Sunday or 'day of the sun' belongs to the first day of the week on astrological grounds, and has long been so used, from *far beyond the Christian era*, and far outside Christian countries.'

"The best possible source for deciding this matter permanently, however, would be a *Babylonian temple text* in which the first day of the week is specifically dedicated to the sun. Such a temple text, translated in detail on pages 71-75 of Sayce's *The Religion of the Ancient Babylonians,* lists each day of the week for an entire month. On the temple text we read:—

'1st day. Dedicated to Anu and Bel (both sun-gods). A day of good luck.... He shall make his freewill offering to the sun, *the mistress of the world*.... He offers sacrifices. The lifting up of his hands find favour with the god.'

'8th day. The feast of Nebo (identified by scholars as being another manifestation of the sun-god).'

'15th day. *Sacred to the Sun*, the Lady of the House of Heaven.'

'22nd day. *Festival of the Sun*, the mistress of the palace.'

'29th day. The day of the resting of the moon-god. The day when the spirits of heaven and earth are adored' (The moon—as also the planets—were considered as an emanation of the sun. The Babylonians had but one god, declares Sayce on page 268 of the book quoted above.)

"In Mithraism, the name by which Babylonian sun-worship was known in Persia, and later in Europe, Sunday, the first day of the week, was the weekly holy day *for centuries preceding Christ*. Likewise in Buddhism the first and fifteenth days of each month are sacred, many Buddhists keeping the intermediate Sundays also, according to Charles Allen Clark in 'Religions of Old Korea,' page 75." Article, "The Counterfeit Memorial," in the Australasian *Signs of the Times*, July 29, 1940.

Sun-day is Babylon's holy day. Many church authorities have openly stated that Sunday observance is not a Biblical practice.

In the Book of Revelation is revealed (as history also informs us) that the religion of Babylon, with Sunday as its holy day instead of the Bible Sabbath, was transferred from ancient Babylon to the Christian church, via Pergamos to Rome. Augustine once expressed the thought that Babylon was, as it were, the first Rome, and Rome, as it were, the second Babylon. However, we should avoid the error into which many Protestants have fallen, namely, of restricting "Babylon" of the Book of Revelation, to Roman Catholicism.

WHAT IS INCLUDED IN "BABYLON" OF THE APOCALYPSE?

"The state of *corruption* and *apostasy* that in the last days would exist in the *religious world*, was presented to the prophet John, in the vision of *Babylon*, 'that great city, which reigneth over the kings of the earth.'... There can be no compromise between God and the *world*." PP 167.

The servant of the Lord has thus interpreted Rev. 17:18 as applying, not to the *literal* city of Rome, but to the *spiritual* city of

Babylon, which is the mystical name and figure for not only the *religious world*, but also for the corruption of the world by sin. The religious apostasy, of course, is specifically referred to as Babylon—but, in its broadest sense, all in rebellion against God are included in Babylon, Satan's kingdom.

We would do well to heed this statement from the Spirit of Prophecy concerning the results following a proper study of the Book of Revelation:—"Especially should Daniel and Revelation have attention as never before in the history of our work. We may have *less to say in some lines, in regard to the Roman power and the Papacy.*" TM 112. This will be so when we see how the whole of the rebellious religious world—whether Roman Catholic or Protestant—is included in God's message against Babylon.

"*The churches*, represented by *Babylon,* are represented as having fallen from their spiritual state to become a persecuting power against those who keep the commandments of God." TM 117. All the churches that will persecute God's Sabbath-keeping people are included in Babylon.

"The term *Babylon* is derived from Babel, and signifies confusion. It is employed in Scripture *to designate the various forms of false or apostate religion.*" GC 381.

When studying concerning the destruction of Babylon, we need to keep in mind what the servant of the Lord has already emphasized, namely, that *all churches are included* (in the final issue, after God's people have been called out of their midst, Rev. 18:4) *in the term Babylon.* Hence less will be said concerning the Papacy being Babylon. Instead of hurling *everything at the Roman power* we shall have to be more comprehensive, and *include all rejectors of the Third Angel's Message.*

"Many of the *Protestant churches* are following Rome's example... and the term *Babylon*—confusion—may be appropriately applied to these bodies." GC 383.

On page 603:—

"The various organizations that constitute Babylon."

TM 61, says:—"The fallen *denominational churches* are Babylon."

See also GC 606:—"In amazement they hear the testimony that *Babylon is the church.*"

The context shows that this includes Protestant churches. See also pages 578, 592, 607, 615; EW 273, 277, etc., where Protestant churches are included in "Babylon," which enforces Sunday laws.

Thus, the servant of the Lord has stressed the necessity of including under the term Babylon all the various organizations which reject the Third Angel's Message. They, *together*, make up *"the mystery of iniquity*, that figures so largely in the winding up of earth's history."

This vast combination of the various organizations of the religious world—Babylon—is brought to view in the Revelation as the final *persecutor* of God's remnant church, and is set forth in the Apocalypse by the *figures* provided by the *various enemies of ancient Israel.* It is necessary to grasp the use of *imagery* in the Revelation—*imagery based upon the experiences of literal, national Israel,* and the overthrow of different enemies who troubled them—in order to understand what is meant by the *symbolical* name "Armageddon." However, as we have dealt with this more fully elsewhere, we will pass on to the further consideration of the fact that apostate Christianity received many of its important festivals from Babylon, though dressing them up in Christian ritualism. As Babylon was the ancient seat of Satan's empire (Isa. 14:4, 12), these festivals were introduced by Satan in his deadly work of opposing the will of God. This is why God's dear heart is grieved when those who profess to serve Him thrust aside the Commandment which plainly admonishes us to "Remember" to keep holy the 7th day, and accept the Sunday of Babylon in its stead.

The Rev. A. Hislop's *The Two Babylons* should be read by everyone. Concerning this book, one says, that it is "the result of the most extensive and scholarly research, and establishes by an *overwhelming mass* of testimony the remarkable fact that *the religion of modern Babylon is derived from ancient Babylon* in Chaldea." On page 2 of his book, Hislop says:—"It has been known all along that Popery was baptized paganism; but God is now making it manifest that the paganism which Rome has baptized is, in all its essential elements, *the very paganism* which prevailed in *ancient literal Babylon.*"

Another book which examines the ceremonies, priesthood, nuns, customs, and practices of Roman Catholicism, and traces them back to old Babylon, says:—

> "The priesthood of Rome... have a true and just claim to be the successors of the pagan priesthood. For not only are the title and office of Pontifex Maximus, and the orders, offices, sacerdotal dresses, symbols, doctrines, sorceries, and idolatries of the priesthood of Rome directly derived from the priesthood

of paganism, but they are the rightful and *direct successors of the supreme pontiffs and priesthood of ancient Babylon and pagan Rome....* On the overthrow of Babylon by the Persians, who nourished a traditional hatred for its idolatry, *the Chaldean priesthood fled to Pergamos*, in Asia Minor, and made it the headquarters of their religion. Hence, Christ in his charge to the church in that city speaks of it as being *'where Satan's seat is.'* (Rev. 2:13.) *The last Pontiff king of Pergamos was Attalus III*, who at his death bequeathed his dominions and authority to the Roman people, 133 B.C., and from that time the *two lines of Pontifex Maximus were merged in the Roman one.* Therefore, when Julius Caesar was elected Pontifex Maximus, he assumed to himself the *divinity* claimed by the pontiff kings of *Chaldea*, and declared himself to be 'Venus Genetrix' or born of Venus, and from *henceforth the emperors of Rome received divine honours.* Moreover, not only had the *serpent* become *the guardian god of Rome,* but *the dragon*, the symbol of him, who, as god of this world, claims the power of bestowing the dominion of the world on whom he will, was adopted as the imperial standard by the emperors, and imperial Rome forthwith became the mistress of the world. Thus, *Satan's seat* and *the center of his power* and authority was finally transferred *from Babylon to Rome."—The True Christ and the False Christ*, J. Garnier, vol. II, p. 85-96.

Surely no one could expect God to look with indifference upon His professing church accepting the festivals of Babylon instituted by Satan! How could God's blessing be upon Sunday observance when, in ancient times, this day was the most important in the worship of the sun? Satan brought Sun-day sacredness into being and particularly into the Christian church, as a counterfeit to the true Sabbath. The great controversy between Christ and Satan has waged down through 6,000 years of human history. Satan changed the Sabbath as part of his devilish plan to turn people away from God's true worship. But, soon, the final conflict will be fought over the true Sabbath. Satan will stir up the whole world to endeavour to force the remnant church to violate the Sabbath Commandment as delivered by God. The Sun-day institution will be made the law of the land, and the heavy hand of persecution will be laid upon those who dare oppose the plan of Satan. In the Book of Revelation we are informed about this great "War" or "Battle." Commencing from Rev. 12:7-9 down to Rev. 20:8, every time the words *"War"* or *"Battle"* are mentioned they refer *only* to the *spiritual* war going on *between Christ and Satan.* This is what God's servant has written so fully about in the "Conflict of the Ages" series—and especially in *The Great Controversy between Christ and Satan.*

Rev. 16:12-16 has *nothing to do with a Palestinian conflict of the nations*—that is an erroneous theory which, *in principle, is opposed to the Third Angel's Message.* Armageddon is the *finale* of the mighty conflict *between Christ and Satan.* Armageddon is a *symbolic* name for the world-wide, overwhelming destruction which is coming to the hosts of Babylon, who, after rejecting God's great Sabbath reform message, *then* are led of Satan to persecute God's people in their endeavour to compel Sabbath-keepers to observe Satan's Sun-day.

CHAPTER IX

Why Did Christ Rise on Sunday, the First Day of the Week?

Having seen what tremendous power is behind sun worship—how it has swayed so much of mankind—how its chief festivals have been made the chief festivals of the professing church of Christ, one naturally enquires, "Why did Christ rise on Sun-day, the first day of the week?" In this act, was Jesus *yielding* to Satan, or *opposing* him? To suggest that He was yielding to the sun-god would be preposterous. Before He died on Calvary He had *refused to yield to Satan's* request to bow to him as his superior. See Luke 4:5-8. No—a thousand times No! *In rising upon the day dedicated to the sun,* Christ, the Lord of the Sabbath day, was not capitulating to the enemy, but He was opposing the work of the evil one. Jesus, in *rising on the sun-day, proved his superiority over the sun god—Satan,* and thus proved that He is the conqueror—"the Invincible Lord."

Satan's original name was Lucifer which means "Day Star." Isa. 14:12. And we are specifically informed by the Infinite Spirit that the pride of Lucifer was engendered by his "*brightness*" which "corrupted (his) wisdom." Ezek. 28:17. His Creator had entrusted him with a "brightness" like a sun, as fitting the greatness of his position as a "covering cherub," verse 16. Instead of this filling his heart with thankfulness for the honour bestowed upon him, he gradually coveted the glory for himself. Only an arrogant selfishness could have thus behaved. His wisdom became corrupted. "The fear of the Lord is the beginning of wisdom." Love of self unbalances the judgment, and makes its possessor do foolish things. When Lucifer, the "Day Star," was transferred to this earth he decided to make the sun—this world's day star—the symbol of his glory, and the first day of the week he selected as the day to bring him honour. It was the day light was created, and it came first, and he would prove that he was first and was superior—"invincible."

We have already seen that God plainly states, in His unerring Word, that sun worship is devil worship. Ps. 106:28, 35-37; 1 Cor. 10:19, 20. When the Jews chose Barabbas—"him that for sedition and murder was cast into prison" (Luke 23:25; John 18:40)—that illustrated the amazing madness of sin. This was also Lucifer's choice in his rebellion against the One who loved him.

Sin is madness—it is suicide. For six thousand years this has been demonstrated upon this earth. "Ye denied the Holy One and the Just, and desired a murderer to be granted unto you; and *killed the Prince (margin, author) of life.*" Acts 3:14, 15.

And how was "the Author of life" killed? Upon the cross which had been for many centuries the symbol of sun worship. Some of the facts in connection with the cross are so shameful that we can only allude to them. The cross was the symbol of the moral corruption of sun worship. To this the writer of the Book of Hebrews refers when he says, "Looking unto Jesus the author and finisher of our faith; who for the joy that was set before Him endured the cross, *despising the shame.*" Heb. 12:2; Eph. 5:12; Rom. 1:18-32.

The "Author of Life," with His form stripped of all its clothing (John 19:23-25; Luke 23:49), hung up before the sun on the symbol of its worship and of its pollution. But God intervened and caused the sun to be darkened. (Luke 23:45; Matt. 27:45; Mark 15:33.) Satan was not permitted to have a complete triumph over Jesus on the cross.

Satan was exultant because Christ was nailed to the cross—the symbol of sun-worship. But, in that hour when he was jubilant that Jesus hung before the face of the "Day Star" (the symbol of his vaunted majesty and supposed invincibility), his doom was irretrievably determined. God's intervention foreshadowed the eventual destruction of the devil, and the ultimate victory of the Lord of glory.

The temporary triumph of the evil one, and Christ's final, complete, and eternal victory, were predicted in the first prophecy ever given. See Gen. 3:15. A similar set of circumstances will occur in the final conflict. Then it will appear that Satan has things as he wishes. The church will suffer through his evil machinations, even as Jesus had sorrow and pain heaped upon Him through the work of God's enemy. In many ways, the remnant church will pass through trials and situations very similar to those through which the Master was obliged to pass. The destruction of the church will seem imminent. Sun-day enforcers, urged on by the same unseen spirits who urged the Jews to reject and crucify the Saviour, will be about to triumph in their design of ridding the earth of God's Sabbath-keeping Israel, when the 6th plague arrests them from accomplishing their murderous plan.

The coming of Christ will quickly follow. (In another place I have considered the time and the chronology involved in the 6th and 7th plagues.) Very little time will elapse from the outpouring of the 6th plague to the end of the 7th plague—most certainly not time enough for a literal gathering of nations in Palestine! Those who have urged the enforcement of Sun-day laws as the way to bring about "peace and safety," are destroyed in "the battle of that great day of God Almighty"—Armageddon.

THE IMPORTANCE OF SUNRISE IN SUN-WORSHIP

To make certain of his victim, the sun god had the grave of the mighty Redeemer sealed with the Roman seal—the Sigillum Solis, or seal of the sun. Matt. 27:66. How could Christ escape? Resting the Sabbath day, as He did at creation, the Saviour waited the coming of the day dedicated to the "invincible sun." A trial of strength was coming. Soon would be revealed who was superior in the great struggle between right and wrong—between the Creator, Omnipotent and Wonderful, and the creature, mighty, but limited in power. The Sabbath passed. Now what would occur? The day anciently dedicated to the sun-god came, and, *at dawn*, wherever the sun was worshipped, its devotees would be praying to the *rising* sun. Let us pause for a while to consider the importance of *sunrise* in the worship of the sun.

> "The Christian festival of Easter also has its solar characteristics. 'The very word Easter,' says Proctor, 'is in its real origin as closely related to the sun movements as the word *east*.'... In Saxony and Brandenburg the peasants still climb the hilltops before the dawn on Easter day to witness the three joyful leaps of the sun, as our English forefathers used to do."—Olcott. *Sun Lore of All Ages,* chap. IX, p. 238.

The Apollo of the Greeks was, perhaps, the greatest of all sun gods. The setting of the sun at nightfall is likened to the crucifixion, and *its rising to the resurrection.* "Thus," says Olcott, "portraying in a startling manner the completeness of the analogy between the lives of Christ and Apollo."

Sunrise was, and is, important to sun worship.

"It was customary to worship the *rising* sun at dawn, at the moment when its *first rays* struck the demons who invade the earth in the darkness. Tacitus describes to us how, at the battle of Bedriacum, in 69 A.D., the soldiers of Vespacion saluted the *rising sun* with loud shouts after the Syrian custom."—*Astrology and Religion,* page 161, by Franz Cumont.

"Nearly all the people of the East, *before the Christian era,* were accustomed *to worship with their faces directed toward the sun rising;* for they all believed that God, whom they supposed to resemble light, or rather to be light, and whom they included within certain bounds, had *His residence* in that part of the heavens *where the sun rises."*—*Institutes of Ecclesiastical History,* book 1, cent. 2, part 2, chap. 4, sec. 1, Murdock's translation.

Terullian, one of the so-called fathers of the church, in his reply to some who accused him of worshipping the sun, said:—

"Others… suppose that the sun is the god of the Christians, because it is a *well-known fact* that we *pray toward the east,* or because we make Sunday a day of festivity…. Do you do less than this? Do not many of you, with an affectation of sometimes *worshipping* the heavenly bodies likewise, move your *lips in the direction of the sunrise?"*

Think of it! Defending a so-called Christian practice because the heathen did likewise!

So far had Satan captured the professing church in his sun-worshipping snare that "in the fifth century, not only heretics, but even faithful followers, were still wont to bow their heads towards its (the *'invincible sun'*) dazzling disc as it *rose above the horizon,* and to murmur the prayer, 'Have mercy on us.'"—*Mysteries of Mithra,* p. 193, by Franz Cumont, Ph.D., LL.D.

The old Mexicans called themselves the "children of the sun," and daily they greeted the rising sun with hymns. The doors of the sun temples of the Incas opened toward the east, so that the *first rays of the sun* fell upon the sun disk with its human face. The ruins of the sun temple in Tehuantepec, Bolivia, show that the *early morning* sun streamed through the entrance into the temple. "At Stonehenge, in England, we find rocks which remind us very much of the rocks of Futami-no-ura, Japan. Also, between these rocks, there can be obtained a most magnificent view of the sunrise," says Alfred Koch in an excellent article in *The Signs of the Times*, May 17, 1928.

In this article on "Sun Worship," the writer also says of some of the people in Japan:—"Standing upright, with hands laid together, and bowed heads, farmers and fishermen eagerly await the appearance of the *rising sun*, worshipping it either in silence or in a low voice."

Jennings says that when the Israelites left Egypt, their custom of commencing the day (at sunset) was in opposition to "The idolatrous nations, who, in honour of their chief god, the sun, began their day at *his rising*."—*Jewish Antiquities*, book 3, chapter 1, p. 297.

The following extract from Mosheim needs very little comment. He says:—

> "Before the coming of Christ, all the Eastern nations performed divine worship with their faces *turned* to that part of the heavens where the sun displays his *rising beams*.... The Christian converts... retained the ancient and universal custom of *worshipping toward the East*."—*Church History*," Cent. 2, part 2, chap. 4, par. 7; Ezek. 8:16.

Commenting on Job 31:26-28, Calmet points out "the custom of adoring the sun at *its rising*."

The custom of sun-worshippers in adoring the sun at *its rising* is brought to view in the experience of Israel shortly after their deliverance from sun-worshipping Egypt. "Israel made a god of gold, a representation of the Egyptian sun god Apis, whose symbol was a bull; and Aaron proclaimed, 'These be thy gods, O Israel, which brought thee up out of the land of Egypt.' And then they evidently proclaimed the day dedicated to the sun god, calling it Jehovah's in the following words: 'Tomorrow is a feast to Jehovah. And *they rose up early* on the morrow [characteristic of sun-worshippers, who adored the sun at its rising], and offered burnt offerings, and brought peace offerings; and the people sat down to eat and to drink, and rose up to play [according to heathen custom; see Morheim's testimony].' Ex. 32:1-7. Thus they 'corrupted themselves.'" See *The Lord's Day, the Test of the Ages*, p. 36, by M.C. Wilcox.

WHAT TIME ON SUNDAY DID JESUS RISE?

Coming back again to the resurrection day we enquire, "What *time* of the day did *Jesus rise?*" Satan would be worshipped as the sun-god at *sunrise*—but *long before sunrise Jesus had risen*. "The first day of the week cometh Mary Magdalene early, *when it was yet dark*, unto the sepulcher, and seeth the stone taken away from the sepulcher." The Roman seal—the seal of the sun—was broken long *before the break of day*. See Matt. 28:1; Mark 16:1-2; Luke 24:1; John 20:1.

The prophet Jeremiah was called to do a great work for God in opposing the worship of the sun, which was practiced so largely by the Jews in his days. Jer. 7:9, 11-18; 8:2; 11:13; 10:2; 19:13; etc. Knowing the tremendous power behind this system, he was afraid. Jer. 1:8. What courage one needs to oppose the world-wide power of Satan's system, which makes itself strong in governmental places, and exercises such power over the nations. Yet God's people have always done this at the risk of death. To encourage Jeremiah in his work, God gave him a vision of an almond tree (v. 11). The almond tree shows its blossom first among the trees—it is before others. "Then said the Lord unto me, Thou hast well seen; for I will *hasten* [a play upon the word 'almond,' which means the hastener] my word to perform it" (v.12). God said to his trembling servant, "Be not afraid of their faces: for I am with thee to deliver thee." We might paraphrase it thus: "You may be sure, Jeremiah, that I will be *first* upon the battlefield. When your enemy comes upon the stage of action he will find Me there, *before him*." And so it was at *the resurrection; Jesus was there first, before the hour of sunrise*.

We are not left to conclude for ourselves that, by His resurrection, Jesus triumphed over Satan the sun-god, for Paul was inspired to express this glorious truth. Writing of Christ's resurrection, the apostle says, "Ye are risen with Him, through the faith of the operation of God, who hath raised Him from the dead. And you... hath he *quickened* together with him." Col. 1:12, 13. In verse 15 we read, "And having *spoiled principalities and powers* [Lucifer had many of high rank in the heavenly world follow him in his rebellion], *He made a show of them openly, triumphing over them in it*."

He made an open show of them and triumphed over them *by rising on the day dedicated to rebellion*, and *He rose before sunrise*, the time particularly set apart for the highest point of that worship.

Christ's resurrection was not only a victory over death and the grave, it was a triumph over Satan and sin—over all that for which Satan's rebellion stood. Sin's wages is death—but sin was before death. Christ's death and resurrection brought victory to righteousness. *Christ had conquered.* He entered into the very stronghold of the evil one, and had won. As Sampson carried to the top of the hill the gates of the Philistine city in which he has been made captive, so Christ burst asunder the bands of death and carried the gates of the grave to the hill of glory, where He now reigns in power. Matt. 16:18; Rev. 1:18. By His resurrection Christ proved that He was stronger than Satan. See Luke 11:22.

The symbol of the death and resurrection of Christ, ordained by God to be perpetuated by the church, is that of baptism by immersion. The candidate closes the eyes, ceases to breathe, and is buried—in imitation of his Lord; then he is raised to "walk in *newness* of life." Then begins a life of victory over sin, Satan, and finally death. Rom. 6:1-9. In Col. 2:12, 13, the *power* following the baptism of the believer is coupled with the *triumphant* resurrection of Christ. v. 15.

Satan, throughout Scripture, is pictured as one of outstanding cunning and craftiness. 2 Cor. 11:3, 13-15. His best work is done in the guise of "an angel of light." Consequently, when Christ arose the first day of the week, Satan influenced people to believe that that day should be observed in honour of Christ's resurrection, knowing all the time that, as the author of rebellion and its day—Sun-day—the glory would really be referred back to himself.

HOW GOD ENDEAVOURED TO TURN ISRAEL FROM SUN-WORSHIP

In the 25th chapter of the Book of Numbers is recorded the shameful failure of Israel on the borders of Canaan. Satan had prepared his plans well. "Israel joined himself unto Baal-peor." "Baal" signified "Lord," the title of the sun god. "Peor" had reference to the locality. Num. 23:28. "And the anger of the Lord was kindled against Israel. And the Lord said unto Moses. Take all the heads of the people, and *hang them up* before the Lord *against the sun*, that the fierce anger of the Lord may be turned away from Israel." Num. 25:1-9 gives the complete story of God's anger, and of the twenty-four thousand who were slain by God for this rebellion against Him. Why did God command that the heads of the sun-worshippers be *hung up against the sun*? Was it to persuade others to worship Baal-peor, the sun-god? A thousand times NO! It was done *to turn people from* having anything to do with sun-worship and its evil ways.

"When the plague of serpents attacked the children of Israel in the wilderness (Num. 21:6-9) God commanded Moses: 'Make thee a fiery serpent, and set it upon a pole.' This pole was evidently a cross, for we read in John 3:14 that 'as Moses lifted up the serpent in the wilderness, even so must the Son of man be lifted up.' The people were to see in the crucified serpent a type of the *work* of Christ, not a type of Christ; it would be strange indeed if God should suddenly start using the universal symbol of the evil one as a symbol of His Son.

"Crucifixion did not originate at Calvary. It was the favourite form of administering the death penalty for centuries before Christ, and was a widespread method of offering human sacrifices to the evil one. When a sun-worshipping general went forth to battle anciently, he was almost sure to offer a multitude of captives to his god, who was in reality Satan. The Behistun inscription tells how three thousand chief Babylonians were crucified at one time as an offering to the sun-god by a Persian general, who had succeeded in capturing them in battle. Alexander the Great is said to have crucified ten thousand as a similar offering after one of his victorious campaigns.

"The cross itself has been sacred to the sun since the dawn of demonology. Look at the sun or at any other bright light through partially closed eyelids, and you will see that the rays of light form themselves into a cross caused by the reflection of the light on the eyelashes and lids. This apparently accounts, according to Olcott, for the cross being used as a symbol of the sun.

"In ancient Babylon art we sometimes find the sun pictured in the sky as a cross rather than a circle.... Go into almost any museum today, and you will find statues of Ra, the Egyptian sun-god, holding the ankh, or ringed cross, in his hand.

"On page 223, of 'A History of Babylon,' by Leonard W. King, is shown a revealing reproduction of an early Egyptian picture. King Akhenaten, with his wife and daughters, is shown on the balcony of his palace. On the headdresses of the pharaoh and the queen is found the sacred serpent, symbol of the evil one, which we find universally connected with sun-worship. Overhead the sun sends out its rays, each of which ends in a hand shown caressing the royal family. Hanging from the sun's disk is a cross, and one of the rays offers a similar cross to the queen....

"It was Christ's death on the cross that sealed Satan's doom. When Satan inspired demon-possessed men to crucify their Creator, he was also crucifying himself in type. Christ came down from the cross; the brazen serpent will never come down....

"God took advantage of the standard means of offering sacrifices to Satan to depict a prophecy of his doom. For centuries men had worshipped the serpent as a symbol of the evil one; they had likewise revered the cross as a symbol of the serpent sun-god, and had crucified human beings upon it as an offering to their demon divinity; now God in type reversed the tables, and put the serpent upon the cross."—Murl Vance in *The Signs of the Times*, September 2, 1940.

Here we have another example of how God took things—the serpent and the cross—belonging to Satan's sun-worship, and used them in order to turn people away from anything belonging to Satan or sun-worship. In Gen. 3:15 the serpent is predicted to first bruise Christ's heel, but Christ would eventually bruise the head of the serpent. That is, the tables would be turned. Satan would have his day, but, later, he would be destroyed. Christ's work of redemption will not be complete until He has destroyed the devil. Heb. 2:14; Lev. 16:21, 22, etc. When the children of Israel were being afflicted by the deadly stings of serpents, the *serpent on the cross* pointed them forward to the time when "that old *serpent*, called the devil and Satan" (Rev. 12:9), would be destroyed in the *final act in the work of the Saviour*. We know, of course, that that destruction will come in the second phase of Armageddon, which transpires at *the end of the millennium*.

Just as God commanded the Israelites to "take all the heads of the people" who had followed the ways of Baal (or sun-worship) "and *hang them up* before the Lord *against the sun*," in order to turn Israel *away* from sun-worship, so He ordered Moses to make "a fiery serpent, and set it upon a pole" (the serpent and the cross—the inseparable factors of sun-worship)—not that we should regard either the cross or the serpent as sacred—but that we should turn from the things of Satan, so that we shall not be destroyed when the time comes for the serpent to have its head bruised.

SUN-WORSHIP ON MOUNTAIN TOPS

Among the places of pilgrimage the tops of mountains are most esteemed, since the worshippers believe that there they are closer to the heavenly gods, and from there the sun appears to be much larger than when viewed from a valley or from a plain. The Olympia of Japan, the Fujiyama, is ascended every summer by tens of thousands of pilgrims for the purpose of worship.

The tops of hills have always appealed to sun-worshippers. They had "their idols round about their *altars, upon every high hill,* in *all the tops of the mountains,*" Ezek. 6:13. "For they also built them high places, and images, and groves, on *every high* hill." 1 Kings 14:23; 2 Kings 17:10; Jer. 2:20; 17:2; etc.

"And the servants of the king of Syria said unto him, Their gods *are gods of the hills; therefore they were stronger than we.*" 1 Kings 20:23. The Psalmist asked the question, "Shall I lift up mine eyes unto *the hills?* whence should my help come? My help cometh from the Lord, which made heaven and earth." Ps. 121:1, 2, margin. Should he look to the hills as the *heathen did* for their help? No! his help came from the Creator.

"Truly in vain is salvation hoped for from the hills, and from the multitude of mountains; truly in the Lord our God is the salvation of Israel." Jer. 3:23.

MOUNT SIN-AI

The worship of the moon god Sin, which centered in Ur of the Chaldees, and which Abram was called by God to leave, was later transplanted to Mount Sinai, giving the mountain its name, according to finds of excavators at Ur. It is significant that that mountain was chosen by God on which to proclaim His law, and that the word which in that language meant idolatry means in our language the transgression of that law. God struck sin in its citadel with His eternal truth.

Of course, God did not proclaim His law upon Mount Sin-ai—the mountain which derived its name from the Babylonian moon god Sin—in order to encourage and perpetuate the worship of the moon god. To the contrary, the Lord proclaimed His law from Mount Sin-ai to point out sin, and to save us from the ways of Satan.

The descendants of Esau were known as Edomites, Idumeans, Temanites, etc. They are pictured throughout the Old Testament as the types of the wicked who will finally be banished forever from God's presence. See Obadiah; Jer. 49:7-22; Isa. 34:1-10. When God proclaimed His righteous law from Mount Sin-ai, He is pictured as coming "from Teman." Hab. 3:3. Compare Deut. 33:2; Judges 5:4, 5; Ps. 68:7. Into the stronghold of idolatry went the Lord of Hosts to proclaim His law against sin. "The earth shook, the heavens also dropped at the presence of God: even Sinai itself was moved at the presence of God, the God of Israel." "The mountains melted from before the Lord, even that Sinai from before the Lord God of Israel." As God shook Mount Sin-ai (dedicated to the moon god Sin) and proclaimed His majesty thereon, so Jesus rose triumphantly on Satan's Sun-day in order to turn people from Satan and his worship.

MOUNT CARMEL

Ahab was the iniquitous king upon the throne of Israel, when Elijah came with heaven's call back to the worship of God. Ahab married "Jezebel the daughter of Ethbaal, the king of Zidonians, and went and served Baal (the sun god), and worshipped him." 1 Kings 16:30-33. How did God work through His servant on that occasion? "Now therefore send, and gather to me all Israel unto *Mount Carmel,* and the prophets of *Baal* four hundred and fifty, and the prophets of the groves four hundred." 1 Kings 18:17-40, tells the complete story of Elijah's challenge to meet the sun-worshipping priests upon their own stronghold—the top of Mount Carmel. The performance of the priests on this occasion gives an idea of the manner in which the sun devotees deported themselves in some of their gatherings. Hear Elijah's mocking of the sun-god's powerlessness. "The invincible (?) sun-god" was defeated upon the place of his strength! Defeated there, that people might turn from sun-worship.

Jesus rose on Sunday, thus demonstrating Himself to be Lord over the instigators of sun-worship—not that people should regard Sun-day as a sacred day, but rather, that they should turn from Satan's false system of worship.

"Thus saith the Lord, Learn ye not the way of the heathen." Jer. 8:2. "Neither shall ye walk in their ordinances." Lev. 18:3. God's people have been specifically warned against the "times" of sun-worship. Lev. 19:26; 2 Kings 21:1-7; Gal. 4:8-10.

The opposite of keeping the "times" of the heathen was to observe God's seventh-day Sabbath. See Lev. 18:2-4; 19:26-28, 30; Ezek. 8:16; 20:12-24; Jer. 7:9, 11-18; 10:2; 17:21-27.

The way to victory is not by worshipping the "invincible (?) sun god," who has been defeated by the Christ, but is found in Jesus, the Creator, Who made the seventh-day Sabbath the sign of His Almighty, Invincible power, and eternal glory.

Christ is the Conqueror! This was again demonstrated when He rose on the day dedicated to the sun.

CHAPTER X

Elijah, Jezebel, Ahab, and the Prophets of Baal—Last-Day Types

Important persons and events definitely associated with *literal* Israel, as recorded in the Old Testament, are *typical* in character. Elsewhere, the writer has considered this important aspect of Biblical exegesis. *Persons* brought to view in the Old Testament *are typical of world-wide movements in the closing days* of earth's history. *Localities* in the Old Testament are also applied in a *world-wide* way in the Apocalypse. When a person, place, or battle mentioned in the Old Testament is applied in the New Testament in a spiritual, or anti-typical world-wide sense, the *whole* of the picture presented in the Old Testament narrative, becomes an *imagery* in the *anti-typical* application—even though all the associated features are not separately applied.

Thus, once we see *Babylon*, the literal city which was built upon the literal river Euphrates, applied spiritually, or anti-typically, as it is in the Apocalypse, then we know that the river Euphrates, in Rev. 16:12, also must be applied spiritually, or anti-typically—which is, of course, world-wide. Things in the *anti-typical* application must *stand together* in the *same relation* as they did in the *literal* setting. So, when our Lord, in Rev. 16, pictured the downfall of spiritual Babylon, we know that His use of the River Euphrates in v. 12, must be applied in the *same anti-typical*, or world-wide sense, as Babylon, which was situated upon that river.

The same principle operates in relation to Elijah and Jezebel. Both of these Old Testament characters are typical. In the Apocalypse there is no *specific* anti-typical application of Elijah to the last message of God now about to sound with its loud cry. By coupling together several verses in the Gospels with Mal. 4:4, 5, we can see the inference of the anti-typical application of Elijah to a world-wide movement, which is to utter its warning message before the final judgments of God fall upon a guilty and unrepentant world. But, the very fact that Rev. 2:20 applies Jezebel, *Elijah's opponent*, in an *anti-typical* sense, is quite sufficient for us to see that all of the factors involved in the Old Testament presentation of the conflict between Elijah and the sun-worshipping forces in his day, are to be anti-typically applied in the last days in connection with the world-wide spiritual conflict. Having drawn our attention to the fact that *Jezebel* is to be understood in an anti-typical sense, the Lord expects us to see that the *whole* of the Old Testament picture is to be *applied in exactly the same way*. Similarly, as all through the Book of Revelation *all* places and designations are employed in a spiritual, or symbolical sense, and that, too, in connection with the battle between the forces of good and evil, it is not necessary to point out that Armageddon is a *symbolical* place. When symbols are employed in the Bible, we are not informed in every instance where the same symbol is used regarding the symbolic interpretation. In fact, in numbers of instances there is nothing to directly indicate that a symbol or a type is employed. In most instances, when once or twice our attention has been drawn to the interpretation of any symbol, we are not directed to the fact again, for it is then left with us to apply the principle whenever we come to the same setting.

Nowhere in Scripture are we instructed that Ahab (the king and husband who introduced sun-worship into Israel to please Jezebel his wife) is typical of the State that will enforce Sun-day keeping, to please the anti-typical Jezebel, the apostate church; but such is the obvious application because of the fact that Jezebel, in Rev. 2:20, is applied by the Lord in an anti-typical manner. An anti-typical application of *one* of the features of the Old Testament narratives is the indication from God—*the principle revealed*—that *all* that is associated with it should also be understood in a world-wide, anti-typical sense.

Elijah and Jezebel clashed in Palestine—in the Megiddo zone. The anti-typical world-wide Elijah, the remnant church, will conflict with the anti-typical Jezebel, the world-wide apostate church, in the anti-typical Megiddo zone. The contest, then, was between Baal, or sun-worship, and the true worship of the God of Israel. Soon the contest will be between apostate religious leaders seeking to enforce the observance of Sunday, and the remnant church, which will stand for the true worship of the God of Israel.

ELIJAH, A TYPE OF THE PEOPLE OF THE THIRD ANGEL'S MESSAGE

Jezebel, working through Ahab, led Israel into idolatry. 1 Kings 16:31-33. Elijah's message proclaimed God's judgment against the apostate people. For three and a half years there was drought—everything became a wilderness. 1 Kings 17:1; 18:1; Jas. 5:17, 18; PK 121-133.

Elijah was blamed for the judgments of God. 1 Kings 18:17; Josh. 7:25; PK 139; GC 590.

The *literal* three and a half years of physical drought had its analogous period in this dispensation of the spiritual and invisible, during the time, times, and a half a time—the three and a half prophetic years—of papal supremacy. Dan. 7:25; 12:7; Rev. 12:6, 14; 13:5. When the Revelator speaks of the apostate church under the figure of a woman, he names that woman "Jezebel." Rev. 2:20-23.

Ahab, the king, representing the power of the State, was influenced and *led by Jezebel*, to lead the nation into idolatry and disobedience. "But there was none like unto Ahab, which did sell himself to work wickedness in the sight of the Lord, *whom Jezebel his wife stirred up*." 1 Kings 21:25; 16:31-33.

So the nations will be influenced and led by "the whore," "Babylon the great"—the *spiritual* leaders—into idolatry and disobedience to God. Jezebel painted her face and attired herself to make a good display (2 Kings 9:30), but that did not prevent her from being hurled from her high position (2 Kings 9:33) through the window to the dust. "The whore—Babylon the Great"—also adorns herself to make a great display (Rev. 17:4; 18:16), but this does not prevent her from being hurled from her high position of queen of the nations. Rev. 18:7, 8, etc. See also Ezek. 16:39 (compare v. 37-39, 41 with Rev. 17:16 where Ezek. 16 forms the basis for the imagery John uses in Rev. 17:16) and Ezek. 23:40.

Jezebel lived with King Ahab in the city of *Jezreel*, where Jezebel afterwards met her horrible death in a sudden manner,

2 Kings 9:30-37. *Jezreel was located in the war-scarred area of Megiddo's ancient battlefield.* The *anti-typical Jezebel* meets her sudden destruction on the battlefield of the anti-typical slaughter of Megiddo—the world-wide destruction of Armageddon.

Elijah was fed miraculously during the drought, 1 Kings 17:3-16. During the time of the world's *spiritual drought* (Amos 8:11-13), which will come after probation closes and also when literal hunger abounds, God's people will be fed by the hand of God. EW 282; GC 629.

"That God Who cared *for Elijah* will not pass by one of His self-sacrificing children. He Who numbers the hairs of their head will care for them, and in time of famine they shall be satisfied. While the wicked are dying from hunger and pestilence, angels will shield the righteous, and supply their wants."—GC 629.

Elijah was supported at the widow's house for "a full year." 1 Kings 17:15, margin. God will preserve His people during the time the plagues are being poured out. Rev. 18:8; Isa. 34:8; 63:4; 26:20, 21; Ps. 91, etc. The widow lived at "Zarephath, which belongeth to Zidon," v. 9. Luke 4:25, 26. It was not safe for Elijah to be found within the sphere of the professing people of God. Christ, too, had to flee to Egypt away from the people who professed to be God's children. Spiritual Israel will become outcasts from the religious world of Babylon. In the hour of test between Elijah and the sun-worshipping priests of Baal, Elijah prayed down *literal* fire from heaven. In the final test, God's people will call down *spiritual* fire—the light of the loud cry. Rev. 18:1; GC 603, 604.

"The power attending the message will only madden those who oppose it. The clergy will put forth almost superhuman efforts to shut away *the light*, lest it should *shine* upon their flocks."—GC 607.

As Satan turns things upside down (Isa. 29:16), he gives that which is *spiritual a literal* application, and so the anti-typical priests of Baal—Sun-day worshippers—will call down literal fire from heaven. Rev. 13:13.

Elijah was blamed for the judgments of God which came upon the disobedient sun-worshippers. 1 Kings 18:17, 18. God's *anti-typical* Elijah—the remnant of Israel—will be held responsible for the judgments of God which are poured out upon the wicked for their disobedience.

"It will be declared that men are offending God by the violation of the Sunday-Sabbath, that this sin has brought calamities which will not cease *until Sunday observance shall be strictly enforced*, and that *those who present the claims of the fourth commandment* thus destroying reverence for Sunday, *are troublers of the people*, preventing their restoration to divine favour and temporal prosperity. *Thus* the accusation urged of old against the servant of God will be repeated, and upon grounds equally well established [1 Kings 18:17, 18 then being quoted]. As the wrath of the people shall be excited by false charges they will pursue a course towards God's ambassadors very *similar to that which apostate Israel pursued toward Elijah.*"—GC 590.

Jezebel sought to slay Elijah, 1 Kings 19:1, 2. The anti-typical, or *spiritual Jezebel*, "the whore, Babylon the great" will seek to destroy the anti-typical, or spiritual, Elijah. Rev. 13:15; 14:20; 17:14, 17. Elijah's message was that they had broken God's commandments (1 Kings 18:18) by following the worship of Baal—the sun. The Third Angel's Message proclaims that Sun-day worship is a part, or a continuation of, Satan's old system of sun-worship, and is opposed to God's commandments. Rev. 14:8-12, etc.

Elijah's work was to restore the true worship of God—the anti-typical Elijah's message is to restore divine things back to their rightful place, Matt. 17:10-13; Luke 1:16, 17; Rev. 7:1-4; 14:6-12, etc.

Elijah was translated to heaven without dying (2 Kings 2:11), and is a *type of the people of the Third Angel's Message*, who will live till Christ comes and be translated without seeing death. Mal. 4:4, 5; Matt. 16:28; 17:1-3, 11; Rev. 14:6-12, 3, etc.

"*Elijah was a type of the saints who will be living on the earth at the time of the second advent of Christ*, and who will be 'changed, in a moment, in the twinkling of an eye, at the last trump,' *without tasting of death*. It was as a *representative of those who shall be translated*, that Elijah, near the close of Christ's earthly ministry, was permitted to stand with Moses by the side of the Saviour on the Mount of Transfiguration. In these glorified ones, the disciples saw in miniature a representation of the kingdom of the redeemed. They beheld Jesus clothed with the light of heaven; they heard the 'voice out of the cloud,' acknowledging Him as the Son of God; they saw Moses, representing those who will be raised from the dead at the time of the second advent; and there also stood *Elijah, representing those who at the close of earth's history will be changed from mortal to immortal, and be translated to heaven without seeing death.*"—PK 227.

Elijah's association with the number 3 in the Scriptures marks him in the Bible's numeric system as having a close relationship *with the people of the Third Angel's Message.* We give a few facts in connection therewith. Elijah was one of the three persons who were on the Mount of Transfiguration. There are three accounts of the Transfiguration: Matt. 17:1-5; Mark 9:2-8; Luke 9:28-36. On this occasion, three miracle-workers who each fasted 40 days and 40 nights, held converse together. God has manifested Himself as the "mighty God" all the way through human history; but it is certainly true that He chose three special periods in which He particularly revealed His power: through Moses and Joshua; later through Elijah and Elisha; the third couplet being Jesus and His apostles. These three periods mark the beginning of epochs in the history of God's chosen.

The fact that Moses fasted 40 days is recorded three times Ex. 34:28; Deut. 9:9, 18. Elijah's wilderness fast is recorded in 1 Kings 19:8, and that of Christ's fast in the wilderness is found in Matt. 4:2. The Holy Spirit shows us that mighty things for God are only done when we set ourselves wholly to the task. Only by fasting and prayer are mighty miracles wrought for God. It is remarkable that following this experience, when Jesus came down from the mount, He found the disciples unable to cast out a devil. This caused Him to say, "This kind goeth not out but by prayer and fasting." Matt. 17:21.

Elijah prophesied that there would be three years' drought. This fact is mentioned three times in the Bible: 1 Kings 18:1; Luke 4:27; Jas. 5:17. When Elijah brought the widow's son back to life "he stretched himself upon the child three times." 1 Kings 17:21. In the third year (1 Kings 18:1) of the three years' drought, which is mentioned three times in the Bible, Elijah met the prophets of Baal on Mount Carmel, and told them to pour water on his altar and on his sacrifice three times. "And he said, Do it the third time. And they did it the third time." 1 Kings 18:34. And in the prayer which followed he said, "Lord God of (1) Abraham, (2) Isaac, (3) and of Israel"; and he used the name Jehovah three times, v. 36, 37.

One fact which should again be emphasized is that, in the Old Testament, it was one man—the *literal* and *typical* Elijah; in the closing days of earth's history it will be an *anti-typical* Elijah—a *world-wide people.* In the Old Testament it was one woman—the *literal* and *typical* Jezebel; in the final struggle it will be an *anti-typical*

Jezebel—a *world-wide religious system*. Then, it was a *literal* husband at the head of the nation who was stirred up by his wife; in the final conflict the Babylonian church will have a *spiritual* husband—the State. See Rev. 17:2, 12, 13; 18:3; 19:2. In the Old Testament Palestine was the territory involved—in the New Testament, and particularly the Apocalypse, the *whole world* is involved.

The final experiences which befell Elijah are also to be duplicated in the experiences of the remnant church—the anti-typical Elijah. Elijah was threatened with death. 1 Kings 19:2. The remnant church will also be threatened with death. Rev. 13, etc. Elijah fled to the mountains. 1 Kings 19:3-8. The remnant people of God will do the same. GC 625, 626. God fed Elijah miraculously. 1 Kings 17:3-6, 9-16; 19:5-8. "God *Who cared for Elijah* will not pass by one of His self-sacrificing children." GC 629. The prophets of Baal were slaughtered after Elijah had completed his work of declaring the true God before the people, and after God had revealed His supremacy. 1 Kings 18:36-40. In the last days, the slaughter of the unfaithful religious leaders will follow the completion of the work of the people of the Third Angel's Message, and after God has revealed His supremacy. The false shepherds will be smitten first. EW 282; GC 656. Elijah was translated shortly after the prophets of sun-worship were slain. 2 Kings 2:11. Similarly, the people of the anti-typical Elijah message will be translated shortly after the false ministers who have enforced Sun-day laws are slaughtered. GC 656, 657.

THE VALLEY OF MEGIDDO— THE TYPICAL PLACE OF CONFLICT

As Jezebel, Ahab, the prophets of Baal, and Elijah are typical, so is the locality where their final conflict was staged, and where, also, the false leaders of religion were slaughtered. The contest between Elijah and his God, and the prophets of Baal and their god (Satan), occurred on Mount Carmel (1 Kings 18:19, 42), which, on account of its proximity to "the valley of Megiddo," some call Mount Megiddo. Notice Dr. Clarke's comment on Rev. 16:16, "But *Mount Megiddo,* that is *Carmel,* is the place according to some, where these armies should be collected."

Of course, it is scarcely necessary to point out that Mount Carmel *is* not Mount Megiddo. *There is no place called Mount Megiddo.*

As I have shown elsewhere, Armageddon is a *symbolic* name. Many years ago, in the days of Dr. Clarke, some believers in the Palestinian Armageddon evidently *suggested* that Mount Carmel *might be taken for granted* as Mount Megiddo *because* there is no place called Mount Megiddo. This is a sample of how men arrive at an erroneous belief even when it is without facts to support it.

In my "What is Armageddon?" I have pointed out that, in Scripture, Megiddo is mentioned as being *in a valley* only (where the river Kishon flows—"the waters of Megiddo."). In 2 Chron. 35:22 and Zech. 12:11 we read of "the *valley* of Megiddo," but we never read in Scripture about *Mount* Megiddo. Armageddon is a symbolic name—a coined word—which combines the mountains of Israel (where, in Ezek. 38, 39, Israel's enemies are pictured as being slain), with "the *valley of Megiddo*," which is mentioned as the place of the destruction of Israel's foes.

I draw the reader's attention to Dr. Clarke's note (in which we see that some in his day had suggested a way out of the impossibility of locating Mount Megiddo by connecting it up with Mount Carmel), only to point out that, comparatively speaking, Mount Carmel is not far removed from "the *valley* of Megiddo."

The prophets of Baal (sun-worship, or devil worship, see Ps. 106:37, 38; 1 Cor. 10:19, 20) who led Israel astray, and who opposed Elijah's message, were brought from the mountain top, "*down* to the brook *Kishon*" (1 Kings 18:40) where they were *all* slain. Elijah had commanded: "Take the prophets of Baal; let *not one* of them escape." The river Kishon came into the picture in the first, fierce conflict between Satan's sun-worshipping forces, and Israel—"by the waters of *Megiddo*... the river *Kishon* swept them away, that ancient river, the *river Kishon*." Judges 5:19-22. That is, in the same valley where *all* the prophets of Baal were slain by "the brook *Kishon*," is also where the sun-worshipping Canaanites (who, under Satan's leadership, fought fiercely against Israel) were all slain. On that occasion, too, "there was *not a man left*." Judges 4:16. "The river *Kishon*" in Judges 5:19-23 is identified as "the waters of Megiddo."

In the typical conflict the Canaanites fought against Israel "by the waters of *Megiddo*." Then, the angels of God came down from heaven to deliver Israel from these sun-worshipping people, who were controlled by "the spirits of devils." See Deut. 18:9-14; Lev. 18:21-28; Judges 4 and 5. These, and other verses, make it clear beyond question that the foes who fought *against Israel* were possessed by *evil spirits*, who urged them on to slay God's people "by the waters of Megiddo." These are some of the historical features which provide the background, or the imagery, employed in the symbolic word "Aramgeddon." In the Apocalypse the picture presented of the final conflict (Rev. 16:13-16) is that of spiritual Israel being attacked by the three sections of Babylon—the dragon (the State), and the beast and the false prophet representing the two apostate sections of Christianity, which use the State to enforce Sun-day laws. This anti-typical Megiddo conflict will be world-wide, and concerns spiritual Israel, who will be protected by angels from heaven as were the Israelites in the first Megiddo battle. Just as *all* the devil-led Canaanites, and all the prophets of Baal were destroyed "by the waters of Megiddo," so all those who in the last days are led by "the spirits of devils" (Rev. 16:14) to persecute and make "war" (Rev. 12:17) on spiritual Israel will be destroyed in "Armageddon—the battle of that great day of God Almighty."

Whatever Old Testament source we use to obtain an illustration of the final battle between the forces of good and evil, the *anti-typical* application is *world-wide*. Esau's march to slay his brother, Jacob; the experiences of Israel in Babylon in the day of the three Hebrew worthies; the plotting to kill Daniel over the law of God; the death decree issued by the Persian king, who was ignorant of the cunning design and jealousy and envy of the bullying dictator Haman in the days of Queen Esther and noble Mordecai; the experiences of Elijah; the defeat of the Egyptians and the triumph of Israel at the Red Sea; the battle of Israel with the kings of Canaan at "the water of Megiddo"; the defeat of the combined foes in the days of Jehoshaphat; the overthrow of the Assyrian army by the power of mighty angels, when they threatened to destroy God's people in Jerusalem; etc.—all these foreshadow and go to make up the complete picture of the last great conflict on the battlefield between truth and error. Like a mighty mountain rising before us, is the fact that *every one* of these things which had a local setting in *literal* Israel's experiences has a *world-wide application in the experiences of spiritual Israel*. *Not one* of these Old Testament incidents is intended to be applied in a *local* manner *again*. There is no "double application" having reference to Palestine or to the literal Jew. The only "double application" which meets the measure given by the Spirit of God is that which takes the *local* things of the Old Testament dealing with the *literal* Jew in the *literal* land of Israel, and, in their second, or "double application," refers them to *spiritual* Israel in the *spiritual* land of Israel-namely, *the whole world*.

If the reference to Megiddo in the coined word "Armageddon" in Rev. 16:16 is interpreted to mean the place of conflict of *nations* fighting *nations*, it would be the only Old Testament place of conflict of Israel and their enemies mentioned in the Revelation to be taken *literally*; the *only* Israel thing, after God's rejection of the Jewish nation, to be applied *locally again* in the whole of the New Testament. And it would also mean that the original purpose of the writing of the Old Testament record, namely, the account of a struggle between *Israel* and an *enemy*, had been lost to view. The reason why the Old Testament gives the history of a conflict "by the waters of Megiddo" is *because* it was a war between God-led *Israel* and the *devil-led hosts opposing them*. If Megiddo were mentioned in the Revelation concerning nations fighting against nations, *then the original purpose for which such record was written would have been lost sight of.*

The Apocalypse is largely made up of allusions to the experiences of ancient Israel and her enemies, all of which are applied *symbolically* in a world-wide sense in predicting the experiences of the church.

The Spirit of Prophecy presents pictures of the future conflicts of the church by referring to the history of Israel. All the prophets of God have worked on the same principle. See Matt. 5:17; 1 Cor. 14:32.

In the Apocalypse, no place, incident, or designation mentioned in the history of *national* Israel, is ever employed to be interpreted as a *literal* place, incident, or designation. The Lord especially drew our attention to "a place called in the *Hebrew* tongue Armageddon," to guide us in applying this as we do all other things belonging to the Hebrews. The belief of the literal gathering of nations to fight other nations at Megiddo, is out of alignment with every Scriptural test by which the Holy Spirit intends we shall know whether a doctrine is true or false.

To meet the unprecedented situation of the near future God has a wealth of light for the remnant church. We need to grasp the meaning of Rom. 15:4, "For *whatsoever* things were written aforetime were written for *our* learning, that we through patience and comfort of the Scriptures might have hope."

How important to the remnant church is the history of the experiences of the Jews—their remarkable deliverances from their enemies by God's protection, as well as *the promises contained in the provisional prophecies regarding Israel*! These are now "*all* for us." (See 6T 410; MH 405). "Now *all* these things happened unto them for *ensamples*" (or "types," margin, see also v. 6 and margin): "and they are written for *our* admonition, upon whom *the ends of the world are come*." 1 Cor. 10:11. In a *special* sense these things belong to the remnant church who live at the time of the final struggle between good and evil. The crisis that is coming is so terrible that God has written much in His word to give the church strength to stand in the unparalleled contest.

The scenes of Israel's past history, recorded for the benefit of the remnant, concerned *local* happenings of a restricted nature; but those thus typified to befall the church are to be of a *world-wide* character. But the results are none the less certain. *Commensurate with the greatness of the opposition and of the universal nature of the situation*, the Infinite God will display His majestic power and glory in the deliverance of His people *from the hand of their Babylonian persecutors*, who will be destroyed in "the battle of that great day of God Almighty," Armageddon.

CHAPTER XI

Will There Be a Period of Peace Just Before Armageddon?

It has been suggested that universal peace will prevail just before Armageddon bursts upon the world. This belief is based mainly on a misunderstanding of 1 Thess. 5:3; Isa. 2:1-6; etc. As is usually the case the wrong view is obtained by interpreting these passages in a "military" sense. Nowhere does the Bible predict a literal gathering of nations to Palestine—neither for military nor religious reasons. Consequently, all ideas based upon this false premise are incorrect. Nothing in the Bible or the Testimonies gives any ground for the assumption that the nations will gather to Jerusalem to crown Satan (who is personating Christ) as king during some peace celebration, to be followed by God's intervention and the slaughter of Armageddon!

The sooner the subject of Armageddon is approached without taking for granted that the Bible teaches a literal gathering of nations to Palestine, the sooner our minds will be prepared to see the truth of this theme.

The combined forces of Babylon will put forth great efforts to build a New World Order. Already we see the "pattern for peace" being advocated by the united efforts of various religious and national organizations. World War No. 1 was declared to be "the war to end war." This time a more determined effort is being exerted. The churches are combining their strength to establish a lasting peace. Leaders of churches are seeking to inculcate Christian principles into the minds of the masses, in order to bring about the hoped-for "Millennium." Many noble men, prompted by sincere desires, are associated with this growing movement. The tragedy of it is that, in not urging the observance of the 7th-day Sabbath, they fail to appreciate the necessity of conforming to the whole of the Decalogue. Only by strict obedience to all of God's Commandments is it possible to establish lasting peace.

Probably there will be some outward measure of success in the endeavour to build a peaceful world. The Scriptures indicate that the Babylonian church will feel confident of success in bringing hope of lasting peace to the world just before the outpouring of God's final judgments. Then, she will say "in her heart, I sit a queen, and am no widow, and shall see no sorrow. Therefore shall her plagues come in one day, death, and mourning, and famine." Rev. 18:7, 8. The Papacy is exerting her power to establish nominal Christianity among the various governments of Christendom. Not understanding the Third Angel's Message, and seeing no other way of saving mankind from disaster, statesmen, politicians, and leaders of Protestant churches are being influenced to believe that the "pattern for peace" is laid down in Papal Encyclicals and teachings, or in co-operating with the Papacy in seeking to bring about better world conditions. While still having some form of belief in distinctive doctrines, but keeping them in the background, different churches are uniting in what they deem the essentials, in the aim to bring about lasting peace. Such a unity or agreement with the "beast" is clearly predicted in Rev. 17:13, 17. The one great doctrine upon which they will have perfect agreement as an essential to the Babylonian scheme of salvation by works, will be the enforcement of Sunday laws. *Trade unions* will also "agree" to this plan, wishing to safeguard the working man's day of rest. In order to answer the question, "Will there be a period of peace just before Armageddon?" let us commence on common ground.

WARS AND OTHER TROUBLES ARE A SIGN OF THE END

When Christ was asked for signs of His coming and of the end of the world, He answered, "Ye shall hear of wars and rumors of wars: see that ye be not troubled: for all theses things must come to pass, but the end is not yet. For nation shall rise against nation, and kingdom against kingdom." Matt. 24:6, 7. Wars would exist down through the years. Before the end came, wars would grow into gigantic struggles involving not only nations, but whole kingdoms.

"All these are the beginning of sorrows," said the Saviour. v. 8. *The Variorum* comment is:—

"Lit. travail pangs, a reference to the phrase 'the pangs of the birth of the Messiah' used by contemporary Jewish theology."

In the margin of the A.V. of Mark 13:7, 8 we read, "The word in the original importeth the pangs of a woman in travail." "The beginning of sorrows, or birth pangs" *will grow in intensity until the kingdom of the Messiah is born.* The remarkable fulfillment of the Saviour's forecast is noteworthy. The greatness of events was to be *the sign of the end.* In harmony with the prediction, the war of 1914-1918 saw the greatest number of nations ever involved in war, with the greatest death roll. Then came the greatest famines, the greatest pestilence, the greatest earthquakes, the greatest floods, the greatest preparations for war; and now [1944] is being waged the greatest war of all. It is the ever-widening circle of these events, which constitute them the signs of the approaching advent. The harbingers of the Saviour's return were to be recognized by their greatness.

"And *great* earthquakes and *fearful* sights and *great* signs." Luke 21:11. "*Great* signs and wonders." "*Great* glory." "*Great* sound of a trumpet." "*Great* voice." Matt. 24:24, 30, 31, margin. "The day of the Lord is *great* and *very* terrible.... The *great* and *terrible* day of the Lord." Joel 2:11, 31. "The *great* day of God Almighty." "There was a *great* earthquake, such as was not since men were upon the earth, so *mighty* an earthquake and so great." Rev. 16:14, 18. According to the prophets the *conditions on earth will get worse and worse*, fluctuating for a time, but, finally, in the midst of the "time of trouble *such as never was* since there was a nation" (Dan. 12:1), Jesus will return to save His people.

The Revelator, prophesying of the last events said, "And *the nations were angry*, and thy wrath is come... shouldest destroy *them which destroy the earth*." Rev. 11:18. Evidently there is destruction abroad when Christ returns to destroy the nations that are destroying the earth.

"THE SPIRIT OF WAR" AMONG THE NATIONS

The servant of the Lord has written:—

"*The world is stirred with the spirit of war.* Soon the scenes of trouble spoken of in the prophecies will take place." 9T 14.

"Fearful tests and trials await the people of God. The *spirit of war is stirring the nations from one end of the earth to the other.* But in the midst of *the time of trouble that is coming....* God's chosen people will stand unmoved. *Satan and his host cannot destroy them;* for angels that excel in strength will protect them." Ibid. 17.

"The spirit of war" is an indication of a *lack of Christian principles;* that *same lack* will also cause the nations to persecute the church—hence the coupling together in the Testimonies of "the spirit of war" among the nations, and their "war" against the remnant church.

"It suits his Satanic majesty well to see slaughter and carnage upon the earth. *He loves to see the poor soldiers mowed down like grass.*" 1T 366.

"*Satan delights in war....* It is his *object to incite the nations to war* against one another; for he can thus divert the minds of the people from the work of preparation to stand in the day of God." GC 589.

These statements indicate that wars will recur till the end, and they will be incited by Satan until he is destroyed. Therefore, while nations will endeavour to obtain peace, and *for a while may seem to have obtained it* yet, in the end, their efforts will be doomed to complete failure. The idea of a successful peace campaign, during which Satan, personating Christ, is crowned at Jerusalem, does not fit in with what is revealed. *If* efforts were made to crown him, it would be by different ones contesting for the honour. If the disciples could quarrel by the side of the world's Redeemer (the Prince and Author of Peace) concerning who would be the greatest in the kingdom, there is no prospect that the world would be at peace for long in the presence of the author of war and bloodshed. Satan's subjects although "united in one object… hate and *war with one another*." 1T 346.

It is not only that Satan stirs the nations to war to keep them from taking time to prepare for eternity, as stated in GC 589, but it is also pointed out in that extract, that "Satan delights in war." And when he has complete control of mankind with the exception of the remnant, he will plunge the *whole world* into *all kinds of trouble* and into indescribable scenes of strife and carnage. "When God shall bid the angels loose the winds, there will be such *a scene of strife as no pen can picture.*" 6T 408.

"*Strife, war, bloodshed*, with famine and pestilence, *raged everywhere.*" 1T 268.

"All the elements of strife will be let loose. *The whole world* will be involved." GC 614. War is only one element of strife—other forms of strife are revolution, anarchy, capital and labour, etc. *"Trade unions* will *be one* of the agencies that will bring upon *the earth* such a *time of trouble as has not been seen since the world began."* Mrs. E. G. White, *General Conference Bulletin*, 1903, p. 200.

"THE SPIRIT OF WAR" INCITES THE NATIONS TO WAR AGAINST GOD AND HIS CHURCH

In this connection notice the following extracts:—

"Everything in our world is in agitation. There are wars and rumours of wars. The nations are angry.... But while already nation is rising against nation, and kingdom against kingdom, there is not now a *general engagement.* As *yet* the four winds are held until the servants of God shall be sealed in their foreheads. *Then* the powers of earth will marshal their forces for *the last great battle.* Satan is busily laying his plans for the *last mighty conflict, when all will take sides."* 6T 14.

Here we notice two ways in which "the spirit of war" is manifested, namely, nations fighting nations, and the conflict over the Sabbath. In these quotations we can see that the war among the nations is not said to be a Palestinian conflict, neither is "the last mighty conflict" over the Sabbath a Palestinian conflict. That the *"last mighty conflict, when all will take sides,"* is over the Sabbath is seen by comparing this statement with the following from 6T 352:—

"The Sabbath question is to be the issue in the *great final conflict* in which *all the world will act a part."* See also 9T 16; etc.

"The great conflict that Satan created in the heavenly courts is soon, very soon to be forever decided. Soon *all the inhabitants of the earth will have taken sides, either for or against the Government of heaven."* 7T 141.

"The conflict that is right upon us will be the most terrible ever witnessed." 6T 407.

These, and other statements in the Testimonies, make it clear that the conflict referred to in these extracts is the *mighty conflict* of *spiritual* forces over God's law.

"We are to see in history the fulfillment of prophecy... to understand the progress of events in the *marshalling of the nations* for the *final conflict of the great controversy."* 8T 307.

Had this extract finished with "the final conflict" it might be concluded that "the marshalling of the nations" pertained to a military war such as is envisaged by the interpretation which presents Rev. 16:12-16 as the marshalling of the nations to Palestine for Armageddon. But this statement from the Spirit of Prophecy shows that, when God's servant uses expressions such as the "*marshalling* of the *nations* for the *final conflict*," she is referring to "the *final conflict* of the *great controversy.*" Such expressions do not have any application to the supposed Palestinian Armageddon. The "marshalling" mentioned in 8T 307 is also mentioned in 8T 49:—

"Already the inhabitants of the earth are *marshalling* under the leading of the prince of darkness; and this is but the beginning of the end."

This, of course, is precisely what is meant in the proper interpretation of Rev. 16:12-16, for, as I have shown in my "What is Armageddon?", the "gathering" or "marshalling of the nations" refers to them *uniting* in a *spiritual* union to war against their Maker and His law. The "marshalling," or uniting is already in progress. "The agencies of evil are *combining* their forces, and *consolidating*. They are *strengthening* for the *last great crisis.*" 9T 11. "Satan *is busily laying his plans for the last great conflict, when all will take sides.*" 6T 14.

In the Greek—"Sunago"—the word for "gather" in Rev. 16:14, and "gathered" in v. 16; Rev. 19:19; etc., is derived from "sun," and the first definition given by Dr. Strong is "union." Hence we see why the Spirit of Prophecy uses the word "*united*" in describing the *spiritual union* of the forces of evil in the coming conflict. That "uniting," "gathering," or "marshalling" has "*already*" commenced, but the union will be absolute and complete *by the time of the 6th plague*, when, as stated in GC 656: "All have made their decisions; the wicked have *fully united* with Satan in his warfare against God... the controversy [or war] is not alone with Satan, but with men."

In GC 561, 562 we read:—"Satan has *long* been preparing for his *final effort*.... He has not yet reached the *full* accomplishment of his designs; but it will be reached in the last remnant of time. Says the prophet... [Rev. 16:13, 14 is then quoted]," which shows that "the battle of that great day of God Almighty," referred to in the texts quoted, comes as the *culmination of events which have preceded it.*

In GC 624, we have another inspired comment on Rev. 16:14:—"*The spirits of devils* will go forth unto the *kings* of the *earth* and to the *whole world* [not to urge them to gather to Palestine!] to fasten them in *deception*, and urge them on to *unite* ["gather" is the word in Rev. 16:14] with Satan in *his last struggle against the Government* of heaven."

Notice also TM 465:—

"Every soul that is not fully surrendered to God, and kept by divine power, will form an *alliance* ["unite" or "gather"] with Satan against heaven, and *join* in battle against the *Ruler* of the universe."

Weymouth's Translation of Rev. 16:14 mentions "the *Ruler* of all," and there can be no doubt that the statement from the Spirit of Prophecy is the divine interpretation of Rev. 16:14.

From these, and other quotations, we can see that, because of their spiritual condition, "the spirit of war" incited by Satan leads nations to fight against each other *in any part of the world*, without any connection with a Palestinian Armageddon. It is the same spirit which will lead them to wage "war" on the remnant church. Such passages of Scripture as Ezek. 38, 39; Joel 3; Zech. 14; Rev. 16:12-16; etc., do not refer to a military war, nor do they *in any way* point to a Palestinian Armageddon, for Armageddon *is the world-wide destruction* which will come to all those who "war" *against God's law and His church*. Great wars are predicted in the Bible and Testimonies, but where the misapplication or misinterpretation comes about is in confusing the prophecies which predict war against the church by applying them to the war of nations. The latter is *never predicted to occur in Palestine*, but the former is couched in a Palestinian setting because the church—spiritual Israel—has taken the place of national Israel, and, as such, *national* enemies of national Israel now apply as *spiritual* enemies of *spiritual* Israel.

In Matt. 24:7, 8 our Lord predicts great wars involving whole kingdoms, and a state of uncertainty shown by there being "rumours of wars"; also "famines, and pestilences, and earthquakes, in *divers places*. All these are the beginning of sorrows."

If these things occurred only in Palestine they would not constitute signs of the end. It is now that they are occurring in "divers places" that we can see them as signs of the end. It is not the Palestinian, but the world-wide nature of these things which constitutes them as signs of the coming King.

However, the church is *represented* as being "in the land of Israel." See such passages of Scripture as Isa. 11:11, 12; 60:1-21; Ezek. 9:1-7; 34:1-31; Ezek. 38, 39; 40-48; Joel 2:1, 15-18, 23, 32; 3:1-17; Zech. 14:2, 3, 12; Ephes. 2:11-13; Rom. 11:26; 1 Pet. 2:5-9; Rev. 11:1, 2; 14:1, 20; etc. The coming of the church out of Babylon (Rev. 18:4) and gathering to the land of Israel is, of course, a *spiritual* gathering, Isa. 11:11, 12; etc. Consequently, being represented as taking the place of literal Israel, national Israel's enemies are now to be understood as the enemies of spiritual Israel, and their warlike gathering to attack spiritual Israel is an imagery representing the perils and the triumphs of the *church*. That is why the Revelator, in describing the coming conflict, speaks of the *symbolical* place where Israel's enemies will be slaughtered as being "a place called in the *Hebrew* tongue Armageddon."

As the church's gathering is a symbolical or spiritual gathering (see also Ephes. 2:21, 22, etc.) to the land of Israel, so the gathering of the nations is also a spiritual gathering.

More is coming upon *the earth* than a supposed-Palestinian Armageddon. Notice the following statement from God's servant:—

> "Everything is preparing for the great day of God... then the wrath of God, which has so long slumbered, will awake.... The desolating power of God is upon *the earth* to rend and destroy. *The inhabitants of the earth are appointed to the sword, to famine, and to pestilence.*" 1T 363.

THE FRENCH REVOLUTION ILLUSTRATES THE TIME OF TROUBLE

How Satan will lead the world during the time he has control of it, may be gauged by the way he swayed men's minds during the French Revolution. These statements from GC 282-288, scarcely need comment:—

> "When the restraints of God's law were cast aside,....the nation swept on to revolt and anarchy.... 'The reign of terror.' Peace and happiness *were banished from the homes and hearts of men*. No one was secure... *Violence* and *lust* held undisputed sway... *atrocities* of an excited and maddened people.... The cities of the kingdom were filled with scenes of horror. *One party of revolutionists was against another party, and France became a vast field for contending masses,* swayed by the fury of their passions. 'In Paris *one tumult succeeded another*, and citizens were divided into a *medley of factions*, that seemed intent on nothing but *mutual extermination.*' And to add

to the general misery, the nation became involved in a prolonged and devastating war with the great powers of Europe."

The frightful scenes of the French Revolution are graphically portrayed in the rest of the chapter. Says the author:—

"All this was as Satan would have it... *his steadfast purpose is to bring woe and wretchedness upon men*... he urges them on to excesses and atrocities... The restraining Spirit of God, which imposes a check upon *the cruel power of Satan*, was in a great measure removed, and he whose *only delight is the wretchedness of men*, was permitted to work his will... the land was *filled with crimes too horrible for pen to trace*."

If this occurred when God's Spirit "was in a great measure removed," what will the whole world be like when Satan has *no restraint* to his cruelties?

THE WORLD UNDER SATAN'S CONTROL!

"The restraint which has been upon the wicked is removed, and Satan has entire control of the finally impenitent.... Unsheltered by divine grace, they have no protection from the wicked one. *Satan will then plunge the inhabitants of the earth into one great, final trouble.* As the angels of God cease to hold in check the fierce winds of human passion, all *the elements of strife* will be let loose. The *whole world* will be involved in ruin *more terrible* than that which came upon Jerusalem of old.... The same destructive power exercised by holy angels when God commands, will be exercised by evil angels when He permits. There are forces now ready, and only waiting the divine permission, to *spread desolation everywhere... strife* and *bloodshed*." GC 614.

When the restraining hand of God is removed strife, bloodshed, and desolation will be "*everywhere*." The wicked *will not combine in a successful peace movement, but eventually will engage in a mad effort of mutual slaughter*, each group striving for the mastery. Notice the following extracts:—

"Satan aroused the *fiercest* and *most debased passions* of the soul. Men did not reason; they were beyond reason—controlled by impulse and blind rage. They became Satanic in their cruelty. In the *family* and in the *nation*, among the *highest* and the *lowest classes alike*, there was *suspicion, envy, hatred, strife, rebellion, murder. There was no safety anywhere.* Friends and kindred betrayed one another. Parents slew their children, and children their parents....

"Satan was at the head of the nation, and the highest civil and religious authorities were under his sway.

"The leaders of the *opposing factions* at times united to plunder and torture their wretched victims, and *again they fell upon each other's forces*, and *slaughtered without mercy*. Even the sanctity of the temple could not restrain their *horrible ferocity*....

"Israel had spurned the divine protection.... Unhappy Jerusalem! rent by *internal dissensions*, the blood of her *children slain by one another's hands* crimsoning her streets *while alien armies beat down her fortifications and slew her men of war.*" GC 28, 29.

"By stubborn rejection of divine love and mercy, the Jews had caused the protection of God to be withdrawn from them, and Satan was permitted to rule them according to his will. The horrible cruelties enacted in the destruction of Jerusalem are a demonstration of Satan's vindictive power over those who yield to his control....

"The Saviour's prophecy concerning the visitation of Judgments upon Jerusalem is to have another fulfillment, of which that terrible desolation was but a *faint* shadow. In the fate of the chosen city we may *behold the doom of a world* that has rejected God's mercy and trampled upon His law.... The records of the past,—the *long procession of tumults, conflicts, and revolutions*, the 'battle of the warrior... with confused noise, and garments rolled in blood,'—what are these, in contrast with *the terrors of that day* when the restraining Spirit of God shall be wholly withdrawn from the wicked, no longer to hold in check the *outburst of human passion* and Satanic wrath! The world will then behold, as never before, *the results of Satan's rule.*" Ibid. 35-37.

Instead of there being a time of actual peace and safety following the enforcement of Sunday laws, the Spirit of Prophecy is decidedly clear that *troubles of all kinds* will multiply right up to the end.

"Soon grievous *troubles* will arise among the nations—*trouble that will not cease till Jesus comes*.... The judgments of God are in the land. *The wars* and rumors of wars, the destruction by *fire* and *flood*, say clearly that the time of trouble, which *is to increase until the end*, is very near at hand." RH, November 24, 1904.

When probation closes and God's protection is withdrawn from the wicked, Satan, who "delights in war," GC 587, "has entire control of the finally impenitent." "Satan will then plunge the inhabitants of the earth into one great, final trouble... *all* the elements of *strife* will be let loose. *The whole world will be involved in ruin more terrible than that which came upon Jerusalem of old... desolation everywhere.*" GC 614.

These extracts make it very clear that *troubles* will increase till probation closes, and *then* Satan will have *entire* control of the world, except the remnant. Instead of him introducing a time of lasting peace he, with his evil angels, will cause all the vilest passions of men to be whipped to a frenzy.

"*The earth* became one *vast field of strife…*" GC 655.

"*Everywhere there is strife and bloodshed.*" GC 656.

The scenes occurring during the overthrow of Jerusalem, and the horrors of the French Revolution, are said to be "*but a faint shadow*"—"in contrast with the terrors of that day when the restraining Spirit of God shall be *wholly withdrawn* from the wicked, no longer to hold in check the outburst of human passion and Satanic wrath! The world will then behold, *as never before, the results of Satan's rule.*" Ibid. 36, 37.

THE SPIRIT OF PROPHECY IS SILENT ON A PALESTINIAN ARMAGEDDON

It may be said, that because Mrs. E. G. White did not lodge any protest against the teaching of a great battle to be fought on the plains of Esdraelon, she, by her silence in the matter, was evidently in agreement therewith. This, surely, is not a reliable method of proving anything. Many are the false theories supported by similar specious reasonings.

We need only remember how the disciples preached about the kingdom being at hand, and yet did not understand what they were preaching. Yet Jesus allowed His disciples to go on preaching something which they did not fully comprehend. The kingdom they envisaged was not the kingdom which Christ meant, when He commanded them to preach it. But Christ allowed them to continue to preach of the coming of the kingdom, even though their idea of it was not correct. Their preaching, though actually not true, served to stir the minds of the people, to agitate them to study the Scriptures concerning the kingdom, and to inculcate in their minds a preparation for it. Thus, despite the blindness of men, the purpose of God was served.

Similarly, in the 1844 movement, God's children preached concerning the commencement of the hour of God's judgment, and yet did not really understand what they preached. The hour of God's judgment which *they* taught was *not the hour of judgment referred to in the prophecy*. In both these instances no voice of a prophet was raised to protest against the preaching of things which were not the actual truth. But, through them, the purpose of God was served in that the minds of men were startled into listening to the voice of God, even though by a message which was not, strictly, Bible teaching. It did, at least, provide an opportunity for the Holy Spirit to speak to the hearts of men to prepare to meet the Divine standards, in readiness for the events which were being proclaimed.

War between nations is one of the fruits of sin, and is one of the ways God punishes nations for their sins. And as sin increases until the end, so will wars increase in intensity, and in the scale of operation.

But the point which must be emphasized is that a *Palestinian "Armageddon" is not once declared in the Spirit of Prophecy.*

This does not mean that Palestine, just as any other portion of the earth, will not become the theater of war. Palestine has its international, as well as its religious importance, and, in the very nature of things, it holds the *possibilities* of becoming a field of conflict. But such scenes of bloodshed as may yet be enacted there will not be "Armageddon."

Error lies in interpreting Joel 3; Ezek. 38, 39; Rev. 16:12-16, etc., as a description of a *military* war and locating it in Palestine.

Men have not grasped all that God has written concerning the final scenes, but, despite that, God has, even through the mistakes of men, been able to stir up the imagination of mankind to expect some colossal event for which they must prepare.

Now that the final scenes are right upon us, it becomes necessary to pay more careful heed to prophetic interpretations. By recent events we can grasp the gigantic nature of upheavals among the nations. In the long ago, when Bible students thought of "the kings of *the earth* and of the *whole* world" gathering to Palestine, they could not conceive of the vastness of modern wars, nor dream of the demands of "total" war, nor the countless thousands of tanks, guns, aeroplanes, ships, etc. In the light of modern warfare, a belief in a literal gathering of "the kings of *the earth* and of the *whole* world" to Megiddo is an absurdity. It is now evident that the coming universal tragedy among the nations, preached by our beloved pioneers, was not, in any sense, overestimated, or exaggerated. Too much emphasis has not been placed upon the coming of a titanic struggle between nations, but the mistake has been in applying as a Palestinian Armageddon those predictions *which really concern the church being attacked by her enemies,* and their world-wide destruction. Let us keep predictions concerning wars between nations *anywhere in the world without specific relation to Palestine,* separate from those predictions which pertain to the final struggle between the forces of good and evil.

THE FAILURE OF PEACE PLANS

We are not left in doubt as to the ultimate failure of plans for a New World Order. God's inerrant Word says, "the ambassadors of peace shall weep bitterly." Isa. 33:7. Whatever achievement for a short time may come to the united efforts of those who are hoping to bring about lasting peace, no matter how rosy the bright prospects of saving mankind from impending doom, swift disaster will follow (1 Thess. 5:3), because, later, the plan for world peace will include the enforcement of Sunday laws. This, of course, will mean bitter persecution for God's people, and then "sudden destruction" will come upon the Babylonian world. Those who would harm the Lord's church—even though actuated by some worldly plan for the benefit of mankind—will receive judgments from God. "For he that toucheth you toucheth the apple of His eye." Zech. 2:8. Never again will the church be obliged to endure a long period of tribulation. Matt. 24:21.

When probation closes all manner of troubles will accompany *the outpouring* of God's *wrath.*

Strife, bloodshed, and commotion will be *"everywhere."* Satan will stir up the wicked against the church, but when at the time of the sixth plague, the crisis has reached its highest peak, God will intervene. The people everywhere will then destroy themselves; and the angels of God will hasten the work of destruction by also slaying the wicked. Isa. 13:3-8, margin; Joel 2:1-11, study with Jer. 51:14, 27; Isa. 33:3, 4; Rev. 9:7; 14:20; 19:14; Zech. 14:13; 1 Sam. 14:15-23; Judges 7:22. As Jehoshaphat and God's people were surrounded by their enemies, and did not have to fight (for God intervened and the angels confused their enemies, who turned on each other and slew until "none escaped"), so will it be with God's people in the valley of God's judgment. 2 Chron. 20:22-27. "The Lord set every man's sword against his fellow throughout all the host"—thus God delivered Israel in the days of Gideon. Judges 7:22. When "the Lord saved Israel" in the days of Jonathan, God employed the same means. 1 Sam. 14:15-23. He has promised to cause the same to be done when the world endeavours to destroy His remnant church. Zech. 14:13; Ezek. 38:21; Hag. 2:21, 22; Isa. 13:8, margin; GC 656; EW 290, etc.

"The Lord... shall strike through the kings in the day of His wrath. He shall *judge among the heathen* [i.e., the *nations* in any part of the world], He shall *fill* the places *with the dead bodies*; He shall wound the heads over *many countries*." Ps. 110:5, 6.

"The Lord shall roar from on high... against *all* the inhabitants of *the earth*.... He will give them that are wicked to the sword... evil shall go forth from nation to nation, and a great whirlwind shall be raised up from the *coasts of the earth*. And the slain of the Lord shall be at that day from *one end of the earth, even unto the other end of the earth*." Jer. 25:30-33. God's judgment—"the valley of Jehoshaphat"—upon the wicked will be world-wide. *The work of slaughter will be world-wide*. Ps. 46:1-10; Dan. 2:43, 44; Isa. 66:15, 16; Isa. 17:12-14; Zeph. 3:8; 1:14-18; Isa. 13:6-13; 28:21; Ps. 2:8, 9; 1 Thess. 5:1-3. "The battle of that great day of God Almighty"(Rev. 16:14) embraces the *whole world*. It is sin's great harvest. Ever since Satan began his rebellion all things have been leading to this great day. Satan, who pretended to be his fellow-creature's friend, is revealed as the murderer of his fellows. Selfishness is shown to be the beginning of murder. Sin is suicide—a world in sin ends by mutual slaughter. Only a universe founded upon love to God and to man can live in happiness and harmony throughout eternity.

Lucifer, the light bearer, commenced his rebellion against God's law on the pretext of improving the status and conditions of his fellow creatures. In his final efforts, in leading the world to "war" against God, and in his attempt to destroy Christ's church he, at first, will hide his real intentions. The argument will be employed that the enforcement of Sun-day laws is necessary for the benefit of mankind, when, all the time, he will be seeking his own exaltation, and the destruction of the people of God.

CHAPTER XII

Sunday Enforcement and the "Peace and Safety" Cry

T he military or Palestinian interpretation of "Armageddon" has, consciously or unconsciously, influenced those who believe in it in their interpretations of other portions of Scripture. One of such passages is 1 Thess. 5:3, which is interpreted to mean that a military peace is to be followed by a military war bringing "sudden destruction." This interpretation leads to the belief that a military peace will exist among the nations before a military Armageddon. But, actually, the "peace and safety" refers to more than freedom from the ravages of war.

In my "What is Armageddon?" we have seen that Micah 4:1-4, and Isa. 2:1-5, are not prophecies of a national "peace and safety" movement, for they refer to Christ's spiritual kingdom now, and to his literal kingdom at the end of the Millennium. While some of their contents may appear to apply to a national peace movement, that is not their true application. One can find many verses from which interpretations may be taken to agree with ideas other than the real objectives of the prophets' messages. Of such are Micah 4 and Isa. 2. Portions are read as though they agree with the idea of a peace movement centered in literal Jerusalem, but other parts of those passages cannot be made to harmonize with the literal interpretation; whereas, the spiritual interpretation blends with every other portion of Scripture.

1 Thess. 5:1-4 informs us of what people will be saying *before* the commencement of the *day of the Lord* when the storm of God's wrath bursts; "For yourselves know perfectly, that the *day of the Lord* so cometh as a thief in the night [i.e., probation closes quietly,

and unannounced]. For when they shall say, *Peace and Safety*; then *sudden destruction* cometh upon them [i.e., the seven last plagues are poured out], as *travail upon a woman* with child; and they shall not escape. But ye, brethren, are not in darkness, that *that day* should overtake you as a thief."

The Scriptures are God's love letter to His church; and, in considering the "peace and safety" cry, we should remember that everywhere the Bible, primarily, refers to "peace" as a spiritual matter—the condition of the soul before God. Far, far too much of the word of God is interpreted as belonging to the temporal realms. The knowledge that God's supreme interest is in His church should be sufficient to cause us to read the Scriptures in the "church" sense first, instead of concluding that certain prophecies (such as Ezek. 38, 39; Joel 3; Zech. 14; Rev. 16:12-16; etc.) refer to military and material things.

General conditions in the world will "wax worse and worse" (2 Tim. 3:13) until religious leaders will be constrained to put forth great efforts to stay the tide of corruption and trouble threatening to end civilization. A prominent feature of the plan to "escape" the threatening "destruction," and to ensure a better state of society—to bring "peace and safety"—will be the enforcement of Sunday laws. Notice the following extracts from GC 587, 589, 614, 615:—

"The enforcement of Sunday observance would greatly improve the morals of society... labouring to promote the highest interest of society.

"It will be declared that men are offending God by the violation of the Sunday Sabbath that *this sin has brought calamities which will not cease until Sunday observance shall be strictly enforced*, and that those who present the claims of the fourth commandment, thus destroying reverence for Sunday, are troublers of the people, preventing *their restoration to divine favour and temporal prosperity.*

"Those who honour the law of God, have been accused of bringing judgments upon the world, and they will be regarded as the cause of the fearful convulsions of nature, and the *strife and bloodshed among men that are filling the earth with woe.*

"It will be urged that the few who stand in opposition to an institution of the church and a law of the state ought not to be tolerated; that it is better for them to suffer than for whole nations to be thrown into confusion.... This argument will appear conclusive; and a decree will finally be issued... to put them to death. Romanism in the Old World, and apostate Protestantism in the New, will pursue a similar course toward those who honour all the Divine precepts."

SUNDAY LAWS BRING GOD'S JUDGMENTS

The nations, by enforcing Sunday laws, will hope to obtain the favour of God, and thus *prevent the increasing troubles on earth.* But this step will prove the sure beginner of greater troubles. Note the message of God from GC 589:—

"The Lord will do just what He has declared that He would do. He will withdraw His blessings from the earth, and *remove His protecting care from those who are rebelling against His law, and teaching and forcing others to do the same.* Satan has control of all whom God does not especially guard."

Again we read from the pen of God's servant:—

"As the angels of God cease to hold in check the fierce winds of human passion, *all the elements of strife will be let loose....* The same destructive power exercised by holy angels when God commands, will be exercised by *evil angels* when He *permits.* There are forces now ready, and *only waiting* the divine permission to spread *desolation everywhere."* GC 614.

Thus, we see that *shortly after the decree enforcing the Sunday-Sabbath, God will withdraw His sheltering hand from the world,* and *"sudden destruction* cometh upon them, as travail upon a woman with child; and *they shall not escape."* This is not a prophecy of the sudden coming of Armageddon, which is associated with the 6th plague, *but of the outpouring of God's judgments at the close of probation,* when "the day of the Lord" comes "as a thief in the night." The day of the Lord begins when the day of salvation ends. 2 Cor. 6:2; Luke 19:42; Zeph. 2:1, 2; Rev. 22:11, 12; etc. Salvation, then, will be no longer possible, for Christ will have completed His work in the heavenly sanctuary. Mercy will no longer be held out to sinners, and God's wrath falls without mixture of mercy. Rev. 14:8-11. *The slaughter of Armageddon* is one of the culminating scenes of the outpouring of His wrath, and *it will be preceded by awful plagues, which begin to fall when the day of salvation ends* and the day of the Lord commences. Paul's statement about people saying "peace and safety," and "sudden destruction" coming upon them, has reference to the close of probation which commences the day of the Lord, and does not specifically refer to (though it later includes) the battle of Armageddon, which is one event—the culmination of previous judgments—in the day of the Lord. While men are having their feasts, quietly as a thief, probation will close as on the night of Belshazzar's festival the bloodless hand wrote the doom of Babylon upon the wall of the king's palace.

THE CLOSE OF PROBATION

Concerning this closing of the door of mercy in the sanctuary in heaven, Christ warns us, "Watch therefore: for ye know not what hour your Lord doth come." Matt. 24:42, 44; 25:13.

"Probation is ended a short time before the appearing of the Lord in the clouds of heaven... men will be planting and building, eating and drinking, all unconscious that the final, irrevocable decision has been pronounced in the sanctuary above.... *Silently, unnoticed as the midnight thief, will come the decisive hour which marks the fixing of every man's destiny,* the final withdrawal of mercy's offer to guilty men. 'Watch ye therefore:... lest coming *suddenly* He find you sleeping.'" GC 490, 491.

"Lest coming *suddenly* He find us sleeping. What time is here referred to? Not to the revelation of Christ in the clouds of heaven to find a people asleep. No; but to His return from His ministration in the most holy place of the sanctuary, when He lays off His priestly attire, and clothes Himself with the garments of vengeance.... He distinctly states the *suddenness* of His coming.... Yet this foretold uncertainty, and *suddenness* at last fails to rouse us from stupidity." 2T 190-192.

The suddenness of the destruction referred to by Paul is the same as that to which the Redeemer refers when he speaks of "coming suddenly," Mark 13:36. Both point to the completion of Christ's work in the day of salvation, and the *sudden commencement of the day of the Lord with the accompanying judgments from God.*

The following references in the Spirit of Prophecy (*Special Testimonies on Education* 107, 108; GC 38, 491; COL 411; PP 104; EW 266; TM 233; etc.) show that 1 Thess. 5:3 has no direct reference to a military "peace and safety" cry followed by "sudden destruction" in merely a military sense, but refers to the close of probation and the commencement of "the *time of trouble,* such as *never was* since there was a nation," Dan. 12:1. "There is no peace, saith my God, to the wicked." Isa. 57:21. Instead of the close of probation bringing a time of "peace and safety" it ushers in this "time of trouble."

In EW 85, we are informed that, *before* the close of probation, *"trouble* will be *coming* on the earth, and the nations will be angry." And the trouble will *increase* when God's mercy is withdrawn and His judgments in the seven last plagues are poured out.

"Soon *grievous troubles* will arise among the nations—*trouble that will not cease until Jesus comes*... the time of *trouble, which is to increase until the end*, is very near at hand." RH, November 24, 1904.

PREPARING FOR "THE BATTLE IN THE DAY OF THE LORD"

"The Lord showed me that a great work must be done for His people before they [not the military] could stand *in the battle in the day of the Lord*.... We [the church] should, therefore, be drawing nearer and nearer to the Lord, and be earnestly seeking that preparation necessary to enable *us* to stand in the *battle* in the day of the Lord." EW 69, 71.

The *battle* to be fought *in* the day of the Lord concerns God's people, for they are to prepare (not in a military sense) by growing spiritually strong to stand in the spiritual conflict.

There will be a work of preparation by both the forces of evil and of good before the close of probation for the "battle in the day of the Lord," Ezek. 13:5. The righteous will receive the fullness of the outpouring of the Spirit in "the latter rain," which enables them to stand through the hour of extreme peril. EW 85, 86, 277. The Devil will be preparing to destroy God's people.

Ezek. 13:5 informs us that, as a preparation for "the house of Israel to stand in the battle in the day of the Lord," the "breach" must be repaired. This work of repairing the breach is plainly stated in Isa. 58:12-14; EW 65-71; etc., to be the Sabbath-reform message. *The false teachers* refuse to repair this "breach"; instead, they *build up "a slight wall"* (Ezek. 13:10, margin), *"saying, Peace; and there was no peace."* Then follows the prediction of God's wrath upon the flimsy wall which will be broken down by the great hailstones. In this chapter we are shown that the Sabbath-reform movement is to be rejected by the false spiritual leaders, and that the *building up by the Papacy, of the Sunday institution—the slight wall—and the daubing of it by the apostate Protestants, is to be followed by the saying of "peace; and there was no peace."* Thus, once more, we are shown that it is *by the enforcement of Sunday observance that Papists and Protestants hope to bring about and preserve peace*. But, *in that very act, they bring sudden destruction upon themselves*. Isa. 30:8-13, presents the same breach made in the wall—the law of God. The false Sabbath-wall will look like a "high wall, *whose breaking cometh suddenly, at an instant*." So we see how, in different places, the Bible makes it clear that Paul's statement, "For when they shall say, Peace and safety; then sudden destruction cometh upon them", refers *to the enforcement of Sunday keeping, soon to be followed by the judgments of God.*

SABBATH KEEPERS BLAMED
FOR INCREASING CALAMITIES

"The great deceiver will persuade men that those who serve God are causing these evils.... It will be declared that men are offending God by the violation of the Sunday-Sabbath, that this sin has *brought calamities which will not cease until Sunday observance shall be strictly enforced*, and that those who present the claims of the fourth commandment, thus destroying reverence for Sunday, are troublers of the people, preventing their restoration to divine favour and temporal prosperity." GC 590.

"*Communications from the spirits will declare that God has sent them to convince the rejectors of Sunday of their error*.... They will lament the great wickedness in the world, and second the testimony of the religious leaders, that the degraded state of morals is *caused by the desecration of Sunday*." GC 591.

"Those who honour the law of God have been accused of bringing judgments upon the world, and they will be regarded as the cause of the *fearful convulsions of nature*, and *bloodshed among men* that are *filling the earth with woe*." GC 614.

"*The day of God* is rapidly approaching. Its footsteps are so muffled that it does not arouse the world from the death-like slumber into which it has fallen. While the watchmen cry, 'Peace and safety,' *sudden destruction* cometh upon them, and they shall not escape." *Special Testimonies on Education* 107, 108.

"Come when it may, *the day of God* will come unawares to the ungodly... then, as the midnight thief steals within the unguarded dwelling, so shall *sudden destruction* come upon [not the military but sinners] the careless and ungodly, 'and *they* [those who rebel against God's law] shall not escape.'" GC 38.

The above quotations show that the sudden destruction to follow the "peace and safety" cry has reference to the *commencement of "the day of God"*—the close of probation and the pouring out of God's wrath in the *seven last plagues*—and is not limited to the pouring out of the sixth and seventh plagues.

"The time is very near when man will reach the prescribed limits.... Wicked *men* and the *church harmonize* this hatred of the law of God, and *then the crisis comes....* Protestants will work upon the rulers of the land to make laws to restore the lost ascendency of the man of sin.... Roman Catholic principles will be taken under the care and protection of the state. *This national apostasy will be speedily followed by national ruin."* Ellen G. White in RH, June 15, 1897, quoted in *The Ministry,* March, 1940.

"This earth has almost reached the place where God *will permit the destroyer to work his will upon it.* The substitution of the laws of men for the law of God, the exaltation, by merely human authority, of Sunday in place of the Bible Sabbath, *is the last act in the drama. When this substitution becomes universal,* God will reveal Himself. He will arise in His majesty to shake terribly the earth." 7T 141.

THE DOOM OF BABYLON FORETOLD IN 1 THESS. 5:3

On examining Paul's statement in 1 Thess. 5:3 and by searching the Old Testament for its source, we discover that it comes from Isaiah's prophecy of the doom of ancient *Babylon.* In Isa. 47, the doom of Babylon is portrayed in unmistakable language, and this is one of the chapters from which John, in the Book of Revelation, quotes in his description of modern Babylon. See verses 7, 8, 9, 11, 14, 15 of Isa. 47, and note the marginal references of Rev. 18. *As literal Babylon trusted in her wickedness (v. 10), and in her counselors led by Satan* (v. 12, 13; also Isa. 44:25) *to avoid the threatened judgments of God, so will spiritual Babylon believe she can prevent the coming world-catastrophe by coercing all to keep Sunday.*

Regarding the wisdom of Babylon's counselors, Isaiah wrote:—"Thus saith the Lord that frustrateth the tokens of the liars, and maketh diviners mad; that turneth wise men backward, and maketh their knowledge foolish," Isa. 44:25. "Stand now with thy enchantments, and with the multitude of thy sorceries… if so be thou mayest prevail. Thou art wearied in the multitude of thy counsels. Let now thy astrologers, the stargazers, the monthly prognosticators stand up, and *save thee from these things that shall come upon thee."* "They shall come upon thee in their perfection for the multitude of thy sorceries, and for the great abundance of thine enchantments," Isa. 47:12, 13, 9. *The disaster* which befell ancient

Babylon came because she used ways forbidden by God as a means of preserving herself—they were the *very cause of her downfall*. This will be repeated in the experience of modern Babylon. Just after the Sunday-enforcement law, the wrath of God will fall upon spiritual Babylon. GC 627, etc.

The prophet Isaiah predicted of ancient Babylon, "But these two things shall come to thee in one day.... Therefore shall evil come upon thee; thou shalt not know from whence it riseth; the mischief shall *fall* upon thee; thou shalt not be able to put it off: and *desolation* shall come upon thee *suddenly*, which thou shalt not know." v. 9, 11.

"Babylon is *suddenly fallen and destroyed*," Jer. 51:8; Jer. 50:44. There can be no doubt that Paul, in writing of the *"sudden destruction"* coming *upon modern Babylon*, had in mind the record of the destruction of the old city of Babylon. Reading again the latter half of 1 Thess. 5:3:—"Then *sudden destruction* cometh upon them, as travail upon a woman with child; and *they shall not escape"*, we see that God is directing our minds to the destruction of literal Babylon as prophesied in Isa. 44, 47, and Jer. 50, 51. *Three statements in 1 Thess. 5:3* definitely connect with the overthrow of *ancient Babylon:*—

1. *"Sudden destruction."* Isa. 47:9, 11; Jer. 51:8; 50:44.

2. *"As travail upon a woman with child."*—"The king of Babylon hath heard the report of them, and his hands waxed feeble: anguish took hold of him, and pangs as of *a woman in travail... suddenly."* Jer. 50:43, 44; see also Isa. 13:1, 6-8.

3. *"And they shall not escape."*—"Mischief shall fall upon thee; *thou shalt not be able to put it off*: and desolation shall come upon thee suddenly." "Let now the astrologers, the stargazers... stand up, and *save thee from these things that shall come upon thee." "None shall save thee."* Isa. 47:11-13, 15. The Babylonians used all their enchantments to their endeavour to save themselves from the threatened ruin. They persuaded themselves that they had succeeded. Their counselors gave assurance that they were safe. But God made "the diviners mad," and frustrated "the tokens of the liars," Isa. 44:25, and the impending judgments came upon them, and *they did "not escape."*

Thus from every angle, we see that when Paul wrote of "sudden destruction" following the "peace and safety" cry, he was not referring to the *suddenness* of a military Armageddon, but to the *sudden closing of probation and the pouring out of the plagues by God, shortly after modern Babylon has tried to preserve civilization from disaster by compelling all to bow to the will of Satan, the author of sun-worship and of Sunday observance.*

"Thus saith the Lord of hosts, the children of *Israel,* and the children of *Judah were oppressed* together: and all that took them captives held them fast; they refused to let them go. *Their Redeemer is strong;* the Lord of hosts is His name; He shall thoroughly *plead their cause,* that He may give rest to the land, and *disquiet the inhabitants of Babylon,*" Jer. 50:33, 34. See PK 532. *The reason for God's overthrow of ancient Babylon* is thus clearly shown to be because the Babylonians *"oppressed"* His people. See also Isa. 14:4.

"Christ identifies His interests with the interests of His faithful people; He suffers in the person of His saints; *and whoever touches His chosen ones touches Him.*" PK 545.

"The Jews had abundant evidence of the literal fulfillment of *Isaiah's prophecy* concerning the *sudden overthrow of their oppressors.*" PK 552.

The whole of Isa. 47, *wherein is foretold the sudden destruction of Babylon,* is quoted in PK 532, 533.

As we have seen, Isaiah 47 is that chapter which Paul particularly refers in his statement in 1 Thess. 5:3, "For when they shall say, Peace and safety, *then sudden destruction* cometh upon them... and they shall not escape." Because ancient Babylon *"oppressed Israel and Judah"* their strong Redeemer brought sudden destruction upon their "oppressors." When modern Babylon oppresses God's last-day Israel by the Sunday-law enforcement, "then sudden destruction cometh upon them." As ancient Babylon trusted in her sorceries and enchantments—*communications from evil spirits*—to escape the impending disasters, but did not escape, so modern Babylon, trusting in "the doctrines of devils"—"communications from the spirits," GC 591—regarding the false Sabbath, and enforcing the Sunday law with the death penalty for its violation, will receive "*sudden* destruction" and "*shall not escape.*"

CHAPTER XIII

Armageddon and the Mark of the Beast

Isaw three unclean spirits like frogs come out of the mouth of the *dragon*, and out of the mouth of the *beast*, and out of the mouth of the *false prophet*. For they are the spirits of devils working *miracles*, which go forth unto the kings of the *earth* and of the *whole* world to gather them to the battle of that great day of God Almighty." Rev. 16:13, 14.

These evil spirits work *miracles*, and thus "*unite*" or gather the *world* to Armageddon. But we are also plainly told that these evil spirits will work *miracles* (through the same Babylonian powers) to bring about the *enforcement of the mark of the beast*. See Rev. 13:12-16. "And deceiveth them that dwell on the earth *by the means of those miracles....* And causeth all... to receive a mark."

This fact is again emphasized in the concluding description of the last great conflict:—"And I saw the *beast*, and the *kings* of the earth, and *their armies*, gathered together to *make war against Him* that sat on the horse, and against His army. And the beast was taken, and with him the *false prophet that wrought miracles* before him, *with which he deceived them that had received the mark of the beast*, and them that worshipped his image." Rev. 19:19, 20.

The *miracles* which lead to the enforcement of Sunday keeping are the *same miracles* (wrought by evil spirits through the Dragon, Beast, and False Prophet) which lead the world to Armageddon. This indicates that Armageddon will come because of the enforcement of Sunday keeping.

By the enforcement of Sunday laws Satan will make "war on the remnant" (Rev. 12:17; GC 592; etc.); that, in itself, will not be

Armageddon, but these laws will bring the church persecution and, later, the threat of death. The attempt to slay God's people because of their allegiance to the Sabbath is the prelude to the slaughter of Armageddon. Through the persecution and threat of death following the passing of stringent Sunday laws, *Satan makes "war on the remnant,"* but "Armageddon is God's *battle"* (the battle... *of God Almighty*) in which He intervenes on behalf of His people, and destroys those who have sought to slay them.

Circumstances surrounding the church will become more and more difficult. The perils will increase. The crisis will come at the time of the 6th plague. The description given by God's servant, in EW 283-285; GC 635-637, applies to the climax hour *just before the outpouring of the 6th plague*, when "every appearance" will be against the church. "It is now, in *the hour of utmost extremity*, that the God of Israel will interpose for the deliverance of His saints." The 6th plague will then be poured out. The waters of the Euphrates which have been flooding over the land of Israel (Isa. 8:7, 8, etc. See "What is Armageddon?" p. 53) are dried up—the people of Babylon (Rev. 17:1, 15) are turned from their murderous intention of destroying God's people by the demonstrations of the mighty power of God exercised on their behalf.

God's servant has written concerning the miracles which lead to the final crisis:—

"Satan has long been preparing for his final effort to *deceive the world*.... Little by little he has prepared the way for his masterpiece of deception in the development of spiritualism. He has not reached the full accomplishment of his designs. But it will be reached in the last remnant of time. Says the prophet: 'I saw three unclean spirits like frogs;... they are *the spirits of devils, working miracles, which go forth unto the kings of the earth, and of the whole world, to gather them to the battle of that great day of God Almighty.*' Except those who are kept by the power of God, through faith in His word, the *whole world* will be swept into the ranks of this *delusion.*" GC 561, 562.

"*Satan* also works with *lying wonders*, even bringing down fire from heaven in the sight of men. (Rev. 13:13). *Thus* the inhabitants of the earth will be brought to take their stand." GC 612.

"*The Protestants of the United States* will be foremost in stretching their hands across the gulf to *grasp the hand of spiritualism*; they will reach over the abyss to *clasp hands with the Roman power*; and under this three-fold union, this country will follow in the steps of Rome in trampling on the rights of conscience. As spiritualism more closely imitates the nominal Christianity of the day, it has greater power to deceive and ensnare. Satan… will appear in the character of an angel of light. *Through the agency of spiritualism, miracles will be wrought*…. Satan determines to unite them in one body, and thus strengthen his cause by sweeping all into the ranks of spiritualism…. *Through spiritualism, Satan appears as a benefactor of the race*, healing the diseases of the people." GC 588-590.

"The *miracle-working* power manifested *through spiritualism* will exert its influence against those who choose to obey God rather than men. *Communications from the spirits will declare that God has sent them to convince the rejectors of Sunday of their error*, affirming that the laws of the land should be obeyed as the law of God…. Great will be the indignation excited against all who refuse to accept their testimony." Ibid. 591.

"*In the soon-coming conflict*, we shall see exemplified the prophet's words: 'The dragon was wroth with the woman, and went to make war with the remnant.'" Ibid. 592.

"Satan… is now putting forth his utmost efforts for a *final struggle against Christ and His followers*…. Antichrist is to perform *his marvelous works in our sight*." Ibid. 593.

It will be seen by these extracts that *the miracles are performed to deceive people regarding the Sunday issue*, and to make the people of God appear to be the ones in rebellion. This causes the world to fall in with Satan's design to bring about the destruction of God's people. *Sunday laws will be enforced, with the death penalty for those who resist the miracles of spiritualism by which Sunday will be shown as the day to be kept*. This is the "war" against the remnant. What is stated on p. 592 of GC to be "the soon-coming conflict" (the war against the remnant), and on p. 593 to be the "final struggle against Christ and His followers" when *miracles* are to be performed by Satan, are associated with the *deceptions* which lead to "*the battle of that great day of God Almighty*" on p. 562.

SATAN PERSONATES CHRIST

"They will perform wonderful *miracles* of healing, and will profess to have revelations from heaven contradicting the testimony of the Scriptures.

"As the crowning act in the great drama of deception, Satan himself will personate Christ…. Now the great deceiver will make it appear that Christ has come…. Then in the assumed character of Christ, he claims to have changed the Sabbath to Sunday, and commands all to hallow the day which he has blessed. He declares that those who persist in keeping holy the seventh day are blaspheming his name by refusing to listen to his angels sent to them with light and truth. This is the strong, almost overmastering delusion. Like the Samaritans, who were deceived by Simon Magus, the multitudes, from the least to the greatest, give heed to these sorceries, saying, This is 'the great power of God.'" Ibid. 624.

Again we see that *the miracles which deceive the whole world and lead them to war against Christ and His followers, are performed to bring about the enforcement of the mark of the beast,* and the consequent destruction of Sabbath keepers—see the next page, GC 625.

"On this *battlefield* comes the *last great conflict* of the controversy between truth and error." 5T 451.

The servant of God so frequently refers to the Sunday-Sabbath issue and the threatened death upon Sabbath-keepers as the *"battlefield"* of "the last great *conflict"*; the "final *struggle* against Christ and His followers"; "the last great *conflict* between truth and error is but the final *struggle*.... Upon this *battle* we are now entering,—a *battle* between the laws of men and the precepts of Jehovah" (GC 582). *The "war" against the remnant is associated with the "battle" or "war"* (both are derived from the same original word) *of Armageddon of Rev. 16:12-16. And the battle of Armageddon is coupled with Rev. 19:11-21,* as may be seen in the following, which quotes from Rev. 19 in referring to "the battle of Armageddon":—

"The battle of Armageddon is soon to be fought. He on whose vesture is written the name, King of Kings, and Lord of Lords, is soon to lead forth the armies of heaven." 6T 406.

In Rev. 19:20, the *miracles* which bring about *the mark of the beast,* and, later, the death penalty on God's people, are thus *associated with the battle of Armageddon.* The miracles are referred to in Rev. 13 in connection with the mark of the beast, and in Rev. 16, as the means Satan employs to bring the nations to Armageddon. *Therefore, Armageddon comes about by the miracles performed by Satan, through Spiritualism, causing the whole world to unite to destroy God's people over the issue of the mark of the beast.*

"The Sunday movement... will reveal the *spirit of the dragon.*" 5T 452.

"*The Sabbath question* is to *be the issue in the great final conflict in which all the world will act a part.*" 6T 352.

"All the world" is to enforce the mark of the beast; "the *whole* world" also takes part in Armageddon! *The same powers are involved in the mark of the beast and in Armageddon,* namely, the dragon (in TM 39, 62, the dragon is said to be the "kings, and rulers, and governors" who enforce Sunday laws), the Papacy, and apostate Protestantism, out of whose mouths come the evil spirits to lead "the kings of the earth and of the *whole world*" to "*the battle* of that great day of God Almighty." *Therefore, the battle of Armageddon cannot be thought of, apart from the mark of the beast.* The *same* powers which enforce Sunday observance under the influence of evil spirits also lead the whole world to Armageddon while under the influence of "the spirits of devils." Armageddon, in other words, will come to those who persecute God's people through the enforcement of Sunday laws.

"Each Sabbath institution bears the name of its author, an ineffaceable mark that shows the authority of each. *It is our work to lead the people to understand this.* We are to show them that it is of vital consequence whether they bear *the mark of God's kingdom, or, the mark of the kingdom of rebellion,* for they acknowledge themselves subjects of the kingdom whose mark they bear." 6T 352.

Bearing the mark of Satan's kingdom—the kingdom of rebellion—the world will march into "the conflict", the "war", "the struggle", "against Christ and His followers", and will meet their doom in the slaughter of Armageddon when God intervenes to deliver His people.

The factors leading up to the final *struggle are invariably* given as the contest between Christ and Satan; between obedience to God as shown in keeping the Sabbath commandment, or obedience to Satan's rule, as shown in observing the false Sabbath. Rev. 12:17; 13:12-17; 14:9-12; 16:2, 10, 12-19; 17:13-18; 19:19, 20.

Satan's effort to compel God's people to obey the Sunday law, and the bitter persecution and attempt to slay them, resulting in the slaughter of the wicked themselves, *are events inseparably linked in Revelation with Armageddon. The same "war" or "battle",* which has waged for 6,000 years, is referred to in Rev. 12:7, 17; 13:15; 14:14-20; 16:12-19; 17:13, 14; 19:11-20; 20:8.

ARMAGEDDON IS THE FINALE
OF THE GREAT CONTROVERSY

"A great crisis awaits the people of God. A crisis awaits *the world. The* most momentous *struggle of all ages* is just before us." 5T 711.

"To secure popularity and patronage, legislators will yield to the demand for a Sunday law. Those who fear God cannot accept an institution that violates a precept of the decalogue. *On this battlefield comes the last great conflict of the controversy between truth and error.*" 5T 451.

"*The Sabbath question* is to be *the issue* in the *great final conflict* in which *all the world will act a part*. Men have honoured Satan's principles above the principles that rule in the heavens. They have accepted the spurious Sabbath, which Satan has exalted as the sign of his authority." 6T 352.

"As America, the land of religious liberty shall unite with the Papacy in forcing the conscience and compelling men to honour the false Sabbath, *the people of every country on the globe will be led to follow her example.*" 6T 18.

"The substitution of the laws of men for the law of God, the exaltation, by merely human authority, of Sunday in place of the Bible Sabbath, is the *last act in the drama. When* this substitution becomes *universal*, God will reveal himself, He will arise in His Majesty to shake terribly the earth." 7T 141.

From the above extracts we see that Sunday laws will first be enforced in America, and "people of *every country on the globe* will be *led to follow* her example" until Sunday laws "*become universal.*" Then God "will arise in his majesty to shake terribly the earth." This, of course, brings us to "the battle of that great day of God Almighty—Armageddon." "The last act in the drama" is not a supposed-gathering of nations to Megiddo, in Palestine, for "Armageddon," but the uniting of the whole world in enforcing Sunday laws to persecute and to slay God's Sabbath-keeping Israel, which results in the world-wide destruction of the enemies of God and His church.

CHAPTER XIV

The Sixth Plague Is for Babylon

That Armageddon should be mentioned in connection with the 6th plague is not without its significance for, in Scripture, the number 6 is *Babylon's* number. On the 6th day of creation the serpent and man were created. Since the fall, man and the serpent are shown in the Scriptures to be working together against their Creator. The 6th Commandment deals with murder. Cain, the first man born into the world, was a murderer, and his genealogy ends with the 6th man. See Gen. 4:17, 18. Cain, at the one end of that genealogy, killed his brother Abel, while Lamech at the other end—the 6th man in the genealogy—also slew a man. Gen. 4:23. In Cain's genealogy is foreshadowed the history of mankind—Cain, the first man, murdered his brother because Abel would not worship God as Cain wished. The 6th plague comes when Babylon has tried to kill the anti-typical Abels who worship God the way He has commanded. The power which will lead out in this work of attempted destruction is branded with the number 666—Babylon's number. See Rev. 13:18.

The 6th clause of the Lord's Prayer deals with sin. In the Bible 6 words are used for man—Adam, Ish, Enosh, Geber (in the Old Testament); Anthropos and Aner in the New Testament. See Bullinger's *"Number in Scripture,"* pp. 154-156. Six times Jesus was charged with having a devil. Mark 3:22; John 7:20; 8:48, 52; 10:20; Luke 11:25.

It is interesting to note that the flood came in the 600th year of Noah's life. Gen. 7:6. The 6th person from the flood in the good line of descendants was Eber. Eber was born 66 years after the flood, in the 666th year of Noah's life (Gen. 11:10-16); and it was during Eber's lifetime that the rebellion of Nimrod came to a head and the confusion of tongues (Babylon) began. *"Unto Eber were born two sons. The name of one was Peleg (that is, 'division'); for in his days was the earth divided."* Gen. 10:25, margin.

LITERAL OR SYMBOLICAL INTERPRETATION?

The image erected by Nebuchadnezzar on the Plain of Dura, was made all of gold, in defiance of Daniel's interpretation of the dream of the Babylonian king. This image was 60 cubits high, and 6 cubits in breadth. Dan. 3:1.

"The numeric value (by gematria) of the words in Dan. 3:1, which describe the setting up of the image is 4462. The very figures are significant, but still more so are the factors of this number—4462=7 x 666."—*Number in Scripture,* p. 285, by Rev. E. W. Bullinger, D.D.

Then, it was a *literal image* erected by the *literal* Babylonians; soon, it will be a *spiritual image* worshipped in spiritual *Babylon.* See Rev. 13:11-18; 14:9, 11; 15:2; 16:2; 19:20; 20:4.

Futurists are literalists, and interpret all the prophecies (which the Third Angel's Message applies to the *whole world*) as belonging to the literal Jews in literal Jerusalem or Palestine. The idea of the battle of Armageddon being waged at, or near Jerusalem, is a *part of Futurism,* which had its origin in Roman Catholicism. See the author's booklet on "Futurism, and the Antichrist of Scripture."

Futurists expect that a literal image to the beast will be erected. They teach that the beast is an individual yet to arise, and to ruthlessly force the Jew (!) in Jerusalem (!) to worship his image! To them, these symbols are not representing *world-wide things,* but they are *limited* to the *Jews* and *Jerusalem,* and the land of Palestine. The idea of a literal conflict between the nations at the literal Megiddo *is simply a part of that system which narrows the world-wide sweep of Israel—predictions* to the literal, limited localities, *as they were in the old Testament typical days.* This very principle itself is sufficient to show that futurism will not fit in with the explicitly revealed keys of prophetic interpretation. Any attempt to narrow down the world-sweep of Bible prophecies is by that very fact proved to be error. To interpret the beast to be an *individual,* and the image to be his *literal* image in Jerusalem, and the three and a half years or 1,260 days to be literal days of the beast's activities in relation to the Jews in Jerusalem, is to take the prophecies concerning spiritual Israel and her enemies and mis-apply them to national Israel and literal Jerusalem. The Third Angel's Message teaches the spiritual application in a world-wide sense, of that which Futurism limits in a *literal* way to the Jews and Jerusalem.

The truth of Armageddon will be readily seen by extending to it the same principle. It concerns Israel, Jerusalem, and the land of Israel, but in a *spiritual,* world-wide sense.

After Israel was established in the Promised Land, the only place where sacrifices could be offered was in the temple of Jerusalem. This is explicitly enjoined in Deut. 12:5-27; 14:23-26; 15:20; 16:5, 6, 15; etc. But the *spiritual* counterpart of the temple services has its application throughout the whole world. Roman Catholicism, having its *literal* wafer, literal water, incense, priests, etc., in a *literal* temple, misunderstands the gift of Calvary. All branches of Babylon make *literal* what is intended by God in His Holy Word, to be world-wide and *spiritual* in application.

The Third Angel's Message shows us that the beast is a symbol of a *spiritual,* world-wide power, and that his *image* and his *mark* are *spiritual* and world-wide in application; and that it is the remnant church—the spiritual Israel in the spiritual Jerusalem—who are involved in the final conflict.

Literalists—futurists—fail to see that as *the image erected in Babylon was literal and local the mention in the New Testament* of the erection of the image in spiritual Babylon shows that it *must* be a *spiritual world-wide image.*

The Book of Revelation, as we have seen, makes use of the historic pictures of the Old Testament and employs them to depict the *spiritual* and final struggles of the church *throughout the world.* In harmony with this principle, the fact of Megiddo being mentioned in the Old Testament shows that its mention in Rev. 16:16 also must be spiritually understood. As the image will be world-wide, so will be the Armageddon slaughter, which results from the attempt to destroy spiritual Israel for refusing to worship the beast and his image.

SPIRITUAL ISRAEL REFUSES TO RENDER HOMAGE TO A SPIRITUAL IMAGE

The three faithful Hebrews who refused to bow to the image of Babylon, represent the people of the Third Angel's Message who will refuse to bow to the *spiritual* image of the beast in *spiritual* Babylon. In *literal* Babylon the people had to *literally* bow before a *literal* image; in *spiritual* Babylon people will *spiritually* bow before a *spiritual* image. What was literal then, is spiritual today.

There cannot be the slightest doubt that John *had the experiences of Shadrach, Meshach, and Abednego before him*, when he wrote of the final scenes regarding the beast and his image. The following facts will help bring this to view. The people in Babylon were to *"worship* the golden *image"* that Nebuchadnezzar had set up. This fact is stated 6 times—Dan. 3:5, 7, 10, 12, 14, 18. In the book of Revelation the fact of *worshipping the beast and his image* is mentioned 6 times—Rev. 14:9, 11; 15:2; 16:2; 19:20; 20:4. (Rev. 13:14, 15 do not *mention* the *worship* of the *beast* and his *image.*)

The 3 men of Israel who would not worship the image are mentioned 6 times as "these men" or "these three men". Dan. 3:12, 13, 21, 23, 24, 27. Their names are given 13 times in connection with the incident of the worship of the image—Dan. 3:12-14, 16, 19, 20, 22, 23, 26, 28-30. They had no part in Babylon's (number 6) rebellion (number 13) in worshipping the image which was erected in defiance of God's interpretation of the image of Dan. 2. In the experiences of these men we are to see the prophecy of the struggle between Israel and Babylon over the image of the beast.

THE THIRTEENTH TIME MEGIDDO IS MENTIONED IN SCRIPTURE

The word "Babylon" occurs 6 times in the Apocalypse. The 6th plague is Babylon's plague, and brings us to Armageddon (Rev. 16:16), which is the 13th (the number of rebellion) time Megiddo occurs in the whole of the Bible. And the word "dragon" also being *found 13 times in the Book of Revelation*, shows that Armageddon is God's answer to a war of *rebellion.*

Judas was the 13th man in the upper room, and lent himself to Satan's plan to kill Christ. In Judas, a professing Christian, leading the religious and pagan world to the betrayal and death of the Son of

God, we see the work of the false prophet, which will lead the religious and worldly elements to war against the remnant church. This attack, however, will end in the slaughter of the *world* thus engaged.

> "The decree which is to go forth against the people of God will be very similar to that issued by Ahasuerus against the Jews in the time of Esther." 5T 450.

We read in Esther 3:7, 12, 13, that the typical decree of death promulgated in the days of Ahasuerus, was issued on the 13th day of the month, and was the 13th year of the king Ahasuerus. It is the anti-typical death decree passed upon modern Israel which results in God's wrath and the consequent slaughter of Megiddo.

WHO IS GOG?

Satan (and, under him, the beast of Rev. 13, etc.) is Gog of Ezekiel 38, 39.

The description given in Ezek. 38, 39 portrays the conflict between Christ and His church and Satan and his vast hordes. *This is the conflict so often spoken of by the prophets, to which Ezek. 38:17 makes explicit mention.* Apart from the direct evidence of plainly stated passages of Holy Writ, the same teaching is sustained by Bible numerics, which is that science of Biblical research which uses "word numbering", as well as the number of times a word, or phrase may be mentioned in Scriptures. Word numbering, stated briefly, is possible because in the Greek and Hebrew languages their system of counting depended upon the letters of the alphabet. Each word, therefore, would have its number value. Gematria is the name given to this word numbering. Some marvelous results have been arrived at by the application of gematria to the names of persons, etc., mentioned in the Bible.

Dr. Bullinger says:—

> "These results may be stated thus, briefly: that the names of the Lord's people are multiples of eight, while the names of those who apostatized, or rebelled, or who were in any sense *His enemies*, are multiples of thirteen." *"Number in Scripture,"* pp. 205, 206.

> "The enemies of God and His people are generally multiples of thirteen".... Satan, in Hebrew, equals 364 (13 x 28). Satan, in Greek, equals 2,197 (13 x 13 x 13)." Ibid. 219.

We see how significant these facts are (and Dr. Bullinger gives many more in his book) in connection with our belief that Ezek. 38, 39 presents *a prophecy of Satan* as the *enemy of God* and *His people,* when we quote the following from the pen of Dr. Bullinger:—

> "Ezekiel's prophecy of Gog—38:2; 'The chief prince of Meshach' (the title of Gog) equals 1,222 (13 x 94); 39:11 'Hamon-Gog' (the burying place of Gog) equals 113. 'All his multitude' equals 156 (13 x 12). The whole prophecy of Ezekiel concerning him (Ezek. 38:2 and 39:29) equals 204256 (13 x 15712). The last portion, 39:16-29 equals 55887 (13 x 4299)." Ibid. 226.

Ezekiel's prophecy concerning "Rosh" or "Gog" is not a vision of Russia attacking the Jews in Palestine, but of *Satan* and his followers *attacking Christ's church*—spiritual Israel—in all the world.

We emphasize, again, that the number 13 is used in Scripture *for rebellion.* Its first use in the Bible, Gen 14:4 shows the meaning attached to it in God's Word. The Dragon, the symbol of Satan in the Book of Revelation, occurs 13 times in that book. And the *13ᵗʰ* time Megiddo is found in the whole Bible is Rev. 16:16, where is described the battle of a *world in rebellion* against God! See Joshua 12:21; 17:11; Judges 1:27; 5:19; 1 Kings 4:12; 9:15; 2 Kings 9:27; 23:29, 30; 1 Chron. 7:29; 2 Chron. 35:22; Zech. 12:11; Rev. 16:16.

Dr. Bullinger in his *The Witness of the Stars,* p. 116, gives the meaning of some of the names of the stars in the constellation of "Perseus":—

> "'The Breaker delivering His Redeemed', The bright star in the left foot is called *Athik, who breaks!* In his left hand he carries a head, which, by perversion, the Greeks called the head of Medusa, being ignorant that its Hebrew root meant *the trodden under foot.* It is also called Rosh Satan (Hebrew), *the head of the adversary,* and *Al Oneh* (Arabic), *the subdued, or Al Ghoul, the evil spirit.*"

This learned author applies the word "Rosh" to Satan, the evil spirit. Dr. Strong says of Hamon-Gog, "The Multitude of Gog; the fanciful name of an *emblematic place in Palestine*:—Hamon-Gog."

The comment in *The Annotated Paragraph Bible* on Ezek. 38, 39 is interesting:—

> "The triumphs of the *church of Christ,* and the *overthrow of its enemies,* are *represented* by the destruction of vast armies of invaders from the extreme north and south (v. 1-6).... But it appears more consistent with the whole scope of scriptural prophecy, and especially with the visions, which immediately follow in chapters 40-48, to give it a more enlarged meaning, understanding it as *describing the consummation of the great conflict* which has always been going *on between the kingdoms of God*

and of Satan in the world, and which will end in the universal establishment of the Saviour's spiritual reign."

Regarding the *Scythians* described in the prophecy, the comment further says:—

"*Vast hordes* of these people made an irruption into Western Asia, *not long before the delivery of this prophecy* (Herod. i. 103-106): and this fact gives peculiar *appropriateness to the selection of them here as the representatives of the combined foes of the church of Christ.*"

Satan, or Gog, leads the combined forces to attack the Israel of God. The formidable army of Ezek. 38, 39 is a picture of a world gathered against the anti-typical Israel.

Armageddon is the destruction of Satan's forces (Gog's great army), the forces of Babylon.

IN BABYLON'S FIERY FURNACE— ANOTHER TYPICAL EXPERIENCE

"The three Hebrews declared to the whole nation of Babylon their faith to Him Whom they worshipped. They relied upon God....

"Important are the lessons to be learned from the experience of the Hebrew youth on the plain of Dura. *In this our day*, many of God's servants, though innocent of wrong-doing, will be given over to suffer....Especially will the wrath of man be aroused against those who hallow the Sabbath of the fourth commandment; and at last a universal decree will denounce these as deserving of death....

"*As in the days of Shadrach, Meshach, and Abednego, so in the closing period of earth's history,* the Lord will work mightily in behalf of those who stand steadfastly for the right. He who walked with the Hebrew worthies in the fiery furnace will be with His followers wherever they are....In the midst of the time of trouble.... His chosen ones will stand unmoved. Satan with all his hosts of evil cannot destroy the weakest of God's saints. Angels that excel in strength will protect them, and in their behalf Jehovah will reveal Himself as a 'God of gods,' able to save to the uttermost those who have put their trust in Him." PK 512, 513.

The fire and the furnace were *literal in literal* Babylon; but they will be *spiritual in spiritual* Babylon. Through that furnace of affliction the loving hand of their God will lead His children to victory and to eternal security.

Louis F. Were

SIX IS BABYLON'S NUMBER

At the dedication of Nebuchadnezzar's image, 6 kinds of music were used. Dan. 3:5, 10, 15. When Belshezzar blasphemed the God of heaven, he praised 6 gods. Dan. 5:4.

The woman, representing the church of Babylon, is mentioned 6 times in Rev. 17:3, 4, 6, 7, 9, 18. Six things are associated with her dress in Rev. 17:4—purple, scarlet, gold, precious stones, pearls, a cup. In Rev. 18:16 the same number is made up as follows:—Purple, scarlet, gold, precious stones, pearls, fine linen.

Six times Babylon is mentioned in the Book of Revelation:— Rev. 14:8; 16:19; 17:5; 18:2, 10, 21. Six times Babylon's "fornication" is referred to:—Rev. 2:21; 14:8; 17:2, 4; 18:3; 19:2.

The voices of 6 persons will not be heard in her again:—Harpers, musicians, pipers, trumpeters, bridegroom, bride. Rev. 18:22, 23.

Six times it is said of the things of Babylon, that they shall be "no more at all." Rev. 18:14, 21-23.

Babylon is "the Mother of harlots and *abominations* of the earth." The Greek word for abomination (bdelugma) occurs 6 times:—Matt. 24:15; Mark 13:14; Luke 16:15; Rev. 17:4, 5; 21:27.

Babylon's Armageddon comes in the 6,000th year of the world. GC 656, 659. Then commences the period of the 1,000 years, which is mentioned 6 times in Rev. 20:2-7. The 1,000 years of desolation being mentioned 6 times, *shows that the destruction is Babylon's. The whole earth* comes under the Babylonian system of rebellion against God. As the slaughter of Armageddon brings the world's destruction, *Armageddon must be Babylon's slaughter, and, consequently, universal.*

In many ways the old sun-worshippers have left their mark upon the world. In our reckoning of time and degrees, the sexagesimal ("pertaining to, or founded on, the number sixty... called also astronomic fractions, because formerly there were no others used in *astronomical calculations*"—Webster) system of reckoning has come to us from worshippers of the fiery orb.

The old sun-worshippers wore an amulet, or charm, upon which was written an ingenious numerical device associating the number 6 with the number 666. The square of six is 36 (6 x 6=36), and the sum of the number 1 to 36=666.

I quote from the pen of the Rev. E. W. Bullinger, in his *Number in Scripture*, p. 286:—

6	32	3	34	35	1
7	11	27	28	8	30
19	14	16	15	23	24
18	20	22	21	17	13
25	29	10	9	26	12
36	5	33	4	2	31

"They may be arranged in the form of a square with *six* figures *each way,* so that the sum of each six figures in any direction shall be another *trinity*—111." (See illustration above.)

One writer says:—"Lenormant informs us that in Egypt, 'The sexagesimal computation was the basis of the whole system of mathematics.' The serpent or crocodile, receiving peculiar veneration and worship, was mystically connected with this number."

"The Egyptian account of this animal was that 60 days elapsed before its eggs were laid; that the eggs were in number 60; that 60 days passed ere they were hatched; that the animals had 60 vertebrae in their spine; that they possessed 60 nerves; that their teeth amounted to 60; that the period of their annual torpidity and fasting lasted 60 days; and, finally, that they obtained the age of 60 years." Wilkinson's *Egypt.*

"Throughout all Egyptian mythology the same numerical system was interwoven. 'Every heathen god,' says Higgins, 'had the name of 666.' Furthermore, the highest symbolism in Egyptian worship and that adopted by the monarchs as the emblem of royalty, was the union of the solar disk and the sacred serpent." Thus, there is a connection between the "sacred" serpent created on the 6th day of creation week, with the worship of the sun, whose number is 6, or 666. Six times 6 makes 36. The numbers 1 to 36, when added together, make a total of 666.

The religion of Egypt combining the solar disk and the sacred serpent became the religion of Rome. The ancient sun amulet, with the unique and mystic total of 666, was adopted as the *Sigillum Solis*, or Solar Seal; while as high priests of the heathen world stood Julius Caesar and his successors, in turn, bearing the title of Pontifex Maximus, which was bequeathed by pagan Rome in the time of Damascus, Bishop of Rome. From the reign of Gratian, Emperor of Rome, who refused the title, the successors in the Holy See have enjoyed both the title and royal costume of Pontifex Maximus. No wonder the Revelator, in prophetically describing the Papacy, says that it would carry the number 666 (the numeric value of the Pope's title—Vicarius Filii Dei—is 666); and wrote the number 666 with the first and the last letters of the Greek word "Christos", with the symbol of the serpent between. The serpent, the symbol of Satan in the Scriptures, is given six names.

The Babylonian sun-worshipping system, with its number 6 (the serpent was created on the sixth day), and the number 666, will meet its complete doom from the time of the outpouring of the 6th plague. The final struggle concerns the mark of sun-worship—Sunday worship—serpent, or devil worship (Rev. 12:9; 20:2; 13:4, 8). This dragon (or the serpent) and Megiddo are associated in the Book of Revelation with the number 13.

The number thirteen in Scripture is not a *national*, but a *spiritual* number—the number of *rebellion against* God.

In Dan. 2, the word "King", when applied *definitely* to Nebuchadnezzar, King of Babylon, is used 39 times, or 3 x 13. The prophetic image of Dan. 2 is of interest to the people of the Third Angel's Message, and is connected with the final struggle of Armageddon. Nebuchadnezzar, the king of *literal* Babylon, was included in the head of the image, and the Pope, the spiritual head of *spiritual* Babylon, in the toes of the feet. That is, located in Europe where the Image is represented as standing. Hence the connection of the 10 toes of the image with the 10 horns of the Papal beast in the closing scenes. Rev. 17:12-18. The 10 toes represent the divisions of the Roman Empire. This means that *the image is represented as standing in Europe* (where spiritual Babylon is centered) *when* Christ, *"the Rock of Ages," strikes the toes* of spiritual Babylon *in the slaughter of Armageddon*. Thus, "the *storm center*" *of God's wrath will not be Palestine* (according to Futurism, or the military interpretation of Armageddon), *but Europe*; or, to be more exact, Rome.

One factor stands out conspicuously—6 is Babylon's number. Babylon has its 3 sections (Rev. 16:19), which, in the widest sense, include the whole of sinful man working with the serpent or Satan. To interpret the *6th* plague, where the *downfall of Babylon is pictured*, as applying to the ending of Turkey or the people living adjacent to the Euphrates, is to spoil the mathematical brand which the Holy Ghost has placed upon the *world-wide Babylon all through* God's Word.

From whatever facet of God's precious jewel, the Word, light shines on the Armageddon question—and one meaning is in all these flashings of the Eternal—*Armageddon is as universal as spiritual Babylon and spiritual Jerusalem*.

As Babylon is world-wide, and as Armageddon brings Babylon's doom, *Armageddon cannot be anything less than the world-wide destruction of the enemies of Christ's church*.

Man and the serpent were both created on the 6th day. For 6,000 years "that old serpent, called the Devil and Satan, which deceiveth the whole world" (Rev. 12:9), has led mankind in its "war" against God. The 6th plague brings us to the time of the awful slaughter of the rebelling, world-wide forces of Babylon.

CHAPTER **XV**

Satan Literalizes the Symbolic Number of the Lord's Resurrection

In the Scriptures the number *eight* is employed as the *symbol* of the Lord's resurrection and triumph over His enemies. This fact is well known to those who have given consideration to the numeric system, which is clearly revealed in the Bible; though there does not appear to have been any attempt made to use this Divinely-given key in the understanding of Armageddon. By employing this key, however, much light is thrown upon the fuller understanding of this important truth. By knowing that the number 8 is the Bible symbol of the Lord's resurrection and triumph over His enemies, we can grasp the meaning of Rev. 17:11, which reads:—"And the beast that was, and is not, even he is the *eighth*, and is of the seven, and goes into perdition."

In the Apocalypse the Lord's enemies are always pictured as having the same things as the Lord—of course, always a counterfeit of, or a resemblance to the things rightly belonging to our Master. Thus, the enemy, as well as our Lord, receives the death stroke, but "his deadly wound was healed: and all the world wondered after the beast." Rev. 13:3. As Jesus was resurrected and triumphed over His enemies, so this power is said to be resurrected to power. This is why Rev. 17:11 refers to "the beast that *was* [i.e., had life and power], and *is not* [lost life and power for a time], even he is the *eighth* [i.e., it is to have a resurrection to life and power]... and goeth into perdition." This persecuting power, even at present, is emerging from its period of powerlessness, and will soon have its dominion restored to it. "The influence of Rome in the countries that once acknowledged her dominion, is still far from being destroyed. And prophecy foretells a *restoration of her power.*" GC 379.

Guided by certain Bible principles (which I have dealt with in the manuscript of my next book, "Armageddon—Before and After the Millennium") we know that this resurrection to power *before the millennium* is a *spiritual* resurrection, whereas it will be a *literal* resurrection at the *end of the millennium.* This organization will have a *spiritual* resurrection to power to engage in a *spiritual gathering* to *a spiritual war;* but, at the end of the millennium, there will be a *literal* resurrection to life and power, a *literal gathering* of the nations around the New Jerusalem to engage in a *literal conflict* against Christ and His church. Rev. 20:8, 9. The first phase of Armageddon (before the 1,000 years) will be a *literal* gathering "to battle." See GC 664.

The Apocalypse presents the number eight as one, and the subject of the millennium as another, of the keys to unlock the doors of difficulty in interpreting all the prophecies concerning Armageddon. This I have shown in my book referred to above. It is enough for our present purpose to say that the first phase of Armageddon takes place at the end of 6,000 years of sin (see GC 659, 673). Then comes the 1,000 years of Rev. 20. Thus, at the end of 7,000 years from creation the second phase of Armageddon will occur. The *8th* millennium brings us to the time of the new world.

Christ's resurrection on Sunday made a certainty of the destruction of His enemies at the end of the millennium. His resurrection proved that He conquers His enemies, and it foreshadows the *complete* conquest of all the wicked, and points to the *new world* which will arise from the ruins of the old in the *8th millennium.* God's enemy, in his endeavour to have Sunday observed as a holy day, makes a wrong use of the significance of the number 8 (as he does with other things of God) in connection with the resurrection of Christ. He has sought to have Sunday of each week called "the eighth day," and has laboured to make the reference to the "eight days" in John 20:26 refer to the first day of the week, as an eighth day, is an attempt to *literalize* the number 8, which is used in Scripture as the symbol of the Lord's triumph over His foes.

THE FIRST DAY OF THE WEEK
MENTIONED EIGHT TIMES

The errors taught under Satan's tuition frequently contain some degree of truth. Christ's resurrection is definitely connected up in the Scriptures with the number 8. For instance, the first day of the week *is mentioned 8 times in the New Testament*: Matt. 28:1; Mark: 16:1, 9; Luke 24:1; John 20:1, 19; Acts 20:7; 1 Cor. 16:2. Thus, the resurrection day of our Lord is mentioned 8 times, because it was the day when He arose in triumph, to a new life. Satan takes the fact of the symbolic use of the number 8 in connection with Christ's resurrection on the first day of the week and uses it to foster his rebellion against God. However, the point to notice is that, while Christ's resurrection day is mentioned 8 times in the New Testament, we are nowhere enjoined to observe that day as a holy day, or to honour that day *every* week. As pointed out earlier, the resurrection fell upon a Jewish *annual* feast day, and there was no need to thrust aside the positive commandment to keep holy the 7th day in order to honour Christ's resurrection *every* week. The service in the old economy, which typified the resurrection (the waving of the first fruits), was enacted once each year; whereas, sacrifices representing the death of Jesus were slain *daily*. As orthodox Christian churches see fit to commemorate Christ's death annually, surely an *annual* event would have been sufficient to commemorate an event which was only prefigured by one annual service in the old economy; whereas, the death of Jesus, which they commemorate *once* a year, was set forth *daily* in the Mosaic economy!

However, the fact remains, that the first day of the week is mentioned 8 times in the New Testament—not that the first day *each week* might be regarded as an eighth day, but because the number 8 is the Bible *symbol* for Christ's resurrection and triumph over His foes and points to His eternal triumph in re-creating—resurrecting a new world out of the ruins of the old world, at the commencement of the 8th millennium from creation.

The New Testament, wherein is recorded the resurrection of Jesus (and the teachings of the gospel regarding the new life in Christ, based upon that wonderful fact), was written by 8 different writers—Mathew, Mark, Luke, John, Paul, James, Peter, Jude.

The Lord's church is symbolized in Rev. 12 as a pure "woman." This church not only believes historically in the resurrection of her Master, but has experienced resurrection power surging through her life, and has found victory over Satan and sin. Therefore, the symbol—the woman—of the church of Jesus is mentioned 8 times in Rev. 12. See verses 1, 4, 6, 13, 14, 15, 16, 17. Thus, the number 8 is a symbol which, with the symbol of the woman, serves as a double check upon our study of this chapter. By this number 8 we know that our conclusions concerning the other features associated with this pure woman are correct. Futurists say that this woman symbolizes *literal* Israel (see Schofield's Bible). But that belief will not harmonize with the number system of Scripture, without considering all the other factors with which it is at variance. The number 8 is not a symbol of *literal* Israel but is the symbol of those who believe in, and *experience*, the *power* of the *resurrection* of the *Lord Jesus Christ*, and who, through Him, triumph over their *spiritual* foes.

As the church of the resurrected One is symbolized by a woman, so the counterfeit church, "the synagogue of Satan" (Rev. 2:9), is symbolized by a woman, but, in contrast to the 8 times the church of the resurrected Saviour is symbolized by the pure "woman" of Rev. 12, the Babylonian impure "woman" of Rev. 17 is mentioned therein 6 times. See verses 3, 4, 6, 7, 9, 18.

Thus, the numeric system of the Bible guides us in our study of the Scriptures. By this way alone (and every other angle of study proves the same), the teaching of a literal gathering of nations to Megiddo in Palestine being "Armageddon," is proved to be an error. My "What is Armageddon?" presents further evidence to support this statement, though, for the fuller application of the number 8 in reference to the second phase of Armageddon, the reader is advised to obtain a copy of *Armageddon—Before and After the Millennium,* which I hope to print shortly.

THE 666 MAN VERSUS THE 888 GOD-MAN

The number of the name of the man who heads up Satan's Babylonian organization is 666. Rev. 13:18. In contrast, the number of the name of Jesus is 888. As the number 666 is made up by counting the numeric value of each letter in the Latin title of the Pope, so the number 888 is made up by counting the numeric value of the Greek letters of the name Jesus.

Circumcision was commanded by God to be attended to on the 8th day (Gen. 17:12). The new life of the baby and the grandchildren to follow were thus dedicated to God. The number 8 thus signified *new* life. The New Testament connects up circumcision with baptism—see Col. 2:11-13. Baptism signifies the burial of the *old* life, and the *rising* to "walk in *newness of life.*" Rom. 6:4. "That *like as Christ was raised up from the dead* by the glory of the Father, even so *we also* should walk in *newness of life.* For if we have been *planted together* in the *likeness of His death,* we shall be also in the *likeness of His resurrection.*" Rom. 6:4, 5.

By this we can see why Peter connects baptism with the flood waters (which brought about a line of demarcation—a complete separation—between the *old* and the *new* world) "wherein few, that is, *eight* souls were *saved* by water, the *like figure* whereunto *baptism* does also now *save* us… by the *resurrection* of Jesus Christ." 1 Pet. 3:20, 21. The 8 souls who were *saved* to walk a *new life* in a *new world* are thus connected up with *baptism,* the symbol of death to the *old* life and a resurrection to the *new* life in Jesus the "888" One. And as we have already seen, baptism, in Col. 2:11-13, is connected up with circumcision which was to be done on the 8th day and was a symbol of the dedication to God of *new* life. The name "Jesus," in the Greek, numbers 888, and He was circumcised on the 8th day. Luke 2:21.

As we all know, the gospel of John sets forth the new life which is to be found in the "Son of God." "Life"—"everlasting life"—is one of the keywords of John. The expression "Son of God" is mentioned 8 times in John's gospel. But the only way this new life in Jesus could come to the sons of men was by the "Son of God" becoming the "Son of man." The term "Son of Man" is applied to Jesus 88 times in the New Testament.

David, a type of Jesus, was the 8th son of Jesse. Solomon, also a type of Jesus, was the 8th son of David. There are 8 steps into the new kingdom:—

Faith	Patience
Virtue	Godliness
Knowledge	Brotherly kindness
Temperance	Charity

"For if ye do *these things,* ye shall never fall: for so an entrance shall be ministered unto you abundantly *into the everlasting kingdom* of our Lord and Saviour, Jesus Christ." 2 Pet. 1:5-11. There are 8 "things" mentioned as being in the new kingdom. See Col. 1:16-20. Eight times Jesus is said to be "in the midst"—the 8th being when the saints are gathered into the new kingdom: Luke 2:46, 47; 4:30; Matt. 18:20; John 19:17, 19; Rev. 1:10-13; 5:6; 7:11-17.

THE SABBATH AND THE NUMBER EIGHT

The Book of Acts shows the church filled with the new life which came to it following Pentecost. That new life was shown in the mighty works they did by the Creator's power—the sign of which is the Sabbath. The Sabbath is mentioned 8 times in the Acts 13:14, 27, 42, 44; 15:21; 16:13; 17:1-3; 18:4.

The adult members of the generation of the Israelites who came out of Egypt failed to enter into their Canaan rest after their toil through the wilderness. When they could have entered the promised land, their hearts were filled with unbelief. From this, Paul, in Heb. 4, in a deeply spiritual application, presents the relation that exists between the *weekly* walk of life and the *Sabbath rest* at the end of the week, with the *pilgrimage of life* which ends (to the enduring, trusting believer) in the *eternal rest* of the everlasting Canaan. Those who learn to rest in the Lord every day of the week are the ones to enter into the proper spirit of Sabbath rest at the end of the week. Those who rest in the Lord throughout the whole of life's desert pilgrimage, will surely enter into the eternal rest after toiling across the wilderness of life.

In writing to the Hebrews of that eternal "rest", Paul uses the Greek word "Katapausis" 8 times. The eighth time points us to the new world, which will be after the resurrection. "Let us labour therefore to enter into *that* rest, lest any man fall after the same example of unbelief." V. 11.

In the book of Hebrews there are 8 "better" things:—

1. Heb. 6:9 Things.	5. Heb. 9:23 Sacrifices.
2. Heb. 7:19 Hope.	6. Heb. 10:34 Substance.
3. Heb. 8:6 Covenant.	7. Heb. 11:16 Country.
4. Heb. 8:6 Promises.	8. Heb. 11:35 Resurrection.

Thus, it is seen that the *eighth* "better" thing in Hebrews is the *resurrection*.

Seven days were occupied in the consecration of the priesthood, and, on the 8th day, they entered upon their work. See Lev. 8:33; 9:1; 14:10, 11. With the cleansing of the leper, too, the 8th day marked a *new beginning*, for on that day he was presented by the priest before the Lord. Lev. 14:9-11.

In Luke 9, we have the record of what Jesus told His disciples of His coming sufferings, and then of a day when He would come in all His glory, v. 26. Then the Sacred narrative presents an inspiring description of the transfiguration of the Lord in the presence of Peter, James, and John, who were privileged to see a wonderful outshining of that predicted glory. Verse 28 says that this took place about *"an eight* days after." Jesus looked past his sufferings to the *new* kingdom illustrated by the transfiguration.

Jehovah made 8 covenants with Abraham: seven before Isaac was offered up, and the *eighth* when he had received Isaac *'in a figure'* from the dead. See Gen. 12:1-3, 7; 13:14-17; 15:13-21; 17:1-22; 18:9-15; 21:12; 22:15-18.

The Rev. E. W. Bullinger, D.D., has written:—

"The use and significance of the number *eight* in Scripture is seen to recur in marvelous exactitude. It may indeed be said that EIGHT is the DOMINICAL number, for everywhere it has to do with the Lord. It is the number of His name Jesus—888." *Number in Scripture, p. 203.*

"Other Dominical Names of Jesus are marked by gematria and stamped with the number eight as a factor:—

> Christ, 1,480 (8 times 185).
> Lord, 800 (8 times 100).
> Our Lord, 1,768 (8 times 221).
> Saviour, 1,408 (8 times 8 times 22).
> Emmanuel, 25,600 (8 times 8 times 8 times 50).
> Messiah, 656 (8 times 82).
> Son, 880 (8 times 110).
>> *–Number in Scripture,* pp. 196-206.

After stating that the number 13, or its multiple, is the number of rebellion, the same writer says:—

> "These results may be stated thus, briefly: That the names of the *Lord's people* are multiples of *eight, while* the names of those who apostatized, or rebelled, or were in any sense *His enemies,* are multiples of *thirteen.*"

From this eminent student of Bible numbers we give another extract dealing with the number eight:—

"The Lord Jesus was on a mountain *eight* times—omitting, of course, the scene in the Temptation. Seven times before the cross, but the *eighth* time *after* He *arose from the dead*.... Abraham's sons were eight in number; but seven were born after the flesh, while one, the *eighth*, was by 'promise.'... The first born was to be given to Jehovah on the *eighth* day (Ex. 22:29, 30).... And it is remarkable that the Bible contains the record of *eight individual resurrections* (other than the Lord and the saints):—

3 in the Old Testament
3 in the Gospels
2 in Acts 9 and 20
=8.

"Eight songs in the Old Testament outside the Psalms:—
1. Redemption, Ex. 15.
2. Supply and maintenance, Num. 21:17.
3. Moses witnessing to the grace of God, and the unfaithfulness of man, Deut. 32.
4. Victory over oppression, Judg. 5.
5. David, God's elect, delivered from all his foes, 2 Sam. 22.
6. The Song of Songs.
7. The song of the well-beloved touching Israel, God's vineyard, Isa. 5.
8. This (the *eighth*) waits to be sung on *resurrection* ground (Isa. 26), for it does not come till after 'death is swallowed up in victory,'" 25:8.

"The miracles of Elijah were *eight* in number, marking the Divine character of his mission:—
1. Shutting up of heaven, 1 Kings 17:1; James 5:17; Luke 4:25.
2. Multiplying the widow's meal, 2 Kings 17:14-16.
3. Raising the widow's son, vv. 17-23.
4. Causing fire to come down from heaven, 1 Kings 18:37, 38.
5. Causing rain to come down from heaven, vv. 41-45.
6. Causing fire to come down from heaven, 2 Kings 1:10.
7. The same, v. 12.
8. Dividing the Jordan, 2 Kings 2:8:"

—*Number in Scripture*, page 202.

TYPICAL EXPERIENCES

Elsewhere, we have shown that the whole of the experiences of Israel were typical of the experiences of spiritual Israel. This, of course, is what is explicitly taught in 1 Cor. 10:6, margin, 11, margin; etc. Their passage across the Jordan has long been seen as the symbol of death—the dividing line between the wilderness journey and entrance into the everlasting Canaan, which, we know, depends upon the resurrection at the second coming of Christ. Elijah's *eighth* miracle was the *dividing of the Jordan*, after which he was translated to heaven. Elijah, as we have shown, is typical of the people who will preach the closing message of God, and who will live till the coming of the Lord. Before God's dear saints are taken to glory the Jordan must first be divided—the power of death must be broken—and then will follow the entrance into Canaan's fair land, to ever be with the Lord.

The Feast of Tabernacles, in the old typical economy, "was the only feast which was kept *eight* days. The *eighth* is distinguished from the seventh. See Lev. 23:39, and compare verses 34-36; Num. 29:39, and Neh. 8:18." As we all know, the Feast of Tabernacles typifies the gathering of all the saved in the New Jerusalem, after the world's harvest has been reaped. "Also in the fifteenth day of the seventh month, *when ye have gathered in* the fruit of the land, ye shall keep a feast unto the Lord seven days: on the first day shall be a Sabbath, and on the *eighth* day shall be a Sabbath." Lev. 23:39. Thus, in the typical service, the first and the *eighth* days (which, recurring *annually*, would come on different days of the *week*) of the Feast of Tabernacles were Sabbaths. They were not typical of the first day of *every week*, for they were entirely independent of, and bore no relation to, the weekly cycle. The anti-type of this typical service belongs to the *new world—after the harvest* which is reaped at the end of the world. See Matt. 13:30, 39; Rev. 14:14-16. The eight-day Feast of Tabernacles will have its fuller application when sin has been entirely banished (as it will be at the end of the Millennium) and the new world begun at the commencement of the 8th millennium from creation.

GATHERING IN THE HEIRS OF THE NEW WORLD

There are 8 miracles, or "signs," in the book of John, namely:—

1. Water turned into wine.
2. Nobleman's son healed.
3. Impotent man healed.
4. Feeding the multitude.
5. Walking on the water.
6. Blind man healed.
7. Lazarus raised.
8. The miraculous catching of 153 fishes, which took place *after Christ's resurrection*. This prefigures the gathering in of all the fish caught in the gospel net. See also Matt. 4:18-20; 13:47-49. According to the latter reference, the fish caught in the gospel net are gathered to the eternal shores at the second Coming of Christ—*after the resurrection*. 1 Thess. 4:16-18.

Eight times Genesis, Chapter 5, records "And he *died*":—verses 5, 8, 11, 14, 17, 20, 27, 31. Death is the prominent feature in "the book of the generation of Adam," verse 1. The only other time that this same expression—"the book of the generation of"—is used in the Bible is Matt. 1:1, where we read of "The book of the *generation of Jesus Christ*." Here we do not read "and he *died*," as in Adam's table of genealogy, but, instead, we find that the word "*begat*" is repeated 39 times. Not *death*, as in the book of the first Adam, but *life—new* life—is stamped throughout the book of "the last Adam." "The last Adam was made a quickening spirit." 1 Cor. 15:45. In "the book of the generation of Jesus Christ," given in the first chapter of Matthew, the fortieth time a new life is born it is that of Jesus. Forty, of course, is 8 times 5. Bethlehem, the place where Jesus was born, is mentioned 8 times in the New Testament.

Rev. 14:14 gives the 88th time "the son of Man" occurs in the New Testament as a designation of Jesus Christ. "The harvest" which He comes to reap at that time—"Ho therimos" in the Greek—has the numeric value, in the gematria of the letters, of 704, which is 8 times 88. We cannot take further space to continue this line of study, but, from what has been presented, one thing is certain—the number 8 is the resurrection number, the number for new life.

The expression *"the Book of Life"* occurs once in the book of Philippians (4:3), and seven times in the Apocalypse—3:5; 13:8; 17:8; 20:12, 15; 21:27; 22:19. Thus, "the Book of Life" is mentioned 8 *times* in the New Testament, which was written by 8 different writers, who wrote 8 times of the fist day of the week—the resurrection day! After the Judgment "the Book of Life" will contain only the names of those who will inherit the *new* world, which is to be created at the commencement of the 8ᵗʰ millennium. Then, the earth will be restored back to its primeval glory—but it will be far more honoured, and more glorious; for "the throne of God and of the Lamb shall be in it." This principle of coming back to where a thing commences is clearly outlined in the Scriptures, and by its use we are able to simplify the understanding of the themes associated with Armageddon, and, by it, the student of Holy Writ is able to be "a workman, that needeth not to be ashamed, *rightly dividing* the word of truth." 2 Tim. 2:15. This principle is enlarged upon in my book, *Armageddon—Before and After the Millennium,* which I hope to publish shortly.

THE NUMBER EIGHT IN THE APOCALYPSE

In the musical world the above-mentioned principle is represented by the octave. The octave brings us back to begin again—only an octave higher—on the same note. This note, which is *eight* above the same note below, has so many more vibrations. And so the repetitions and the anti-types of prophetic imagery (with which the Revelation is replete) are always magnifications of the historical basis upon which they rest.

In Rev. 1 there is employed an Epanados, which serves to illustrate the law of repetition whereby the last comes back to the first, but on a higher note, or greater number of vibrations, if we regard it in the terms of the octave. Of course, these things are always used to exalt Jesus—for it is "The Revelation of Jesus Christ."

In Rev. 1 *eight* quotations from the Old Testament are used in exalting Jesus as the destroyer of His enemies and the Deliverer of His people. These *eight* texts are so employed that the first text is quoted from the same Old Testament book as the *eighth*, and keeping before us the principle of "the *first* and the *last*," we note that the second Old Testament quotation is from the same book as the second to last; the third from the same book as the third from last; and the central ones—the fourth from the first and fourth from the last—are from the same Old Testament book. The following sets forth this Epanados, employed in Rev. 1 to declare Christ's Lordship:—

    (1) V. 5. Isa. 55:4.
      (2) V. 7. Dan. 7:13.
        (3) V. 7. Zech. 12:10.
          (4) V. 8. Isa. 41:4; 44:6; 48:12.
          (4) V. 11. Isa. 41:4; 44:6; 48:12.
        (3) V. 12. Zech. 4:2.
      (2) V. 13-15. Dan. 7:9, 13, 22; 10:5, 6.
    (1) V. 16. Isa. 49:2.

Our Lord, in setting forth the truth that He is "the first and the last," employed this Epanados as one of the means of arresting our attention so that we would study such laws of interpretation as the law of repetition, which is based upon the ascending scale; the law of types and anti-types, which brings us back again to where things were before, but in a spiritual, world-wide sense; the law of the first and the last, etc. This Epanados shows, too, the importance of the number 8 as the *symbol* of the Lord's power and victory in the destruction of His enemies, and His Almighty power to save His people.

The *first* quotation in this Epanados, like the *eighth*—which is the last—is *from the book of Isaiah*. The *first* text from Isaiah (55:4) says that the Messiah would be "a *Leader* and a *Commander* to the people." The eighth (and last) quotation in this Epanados, in bringing us back to Isaiah (49:2) shows *how* the Lord proves to be the "Leader and Commander to the people."

"*Out of His mouth went a two-edged sword.*" Rev. 1:16. The destruction of His enemies by the sword of His mouth, referred to in Isa. 49:2, which is the *8th* text quoted in the Epanados of Rev. 1, is again repeated (according to the law of repetition, which is the law of explanation) in Rev. 19:15, 21:—"*Out of His mouth goeth a sharp sword, that with it He should smite the nations.*" Christ destroys His enemies at His second coming—that coming and that destruction will affect the whole world.

Many verses from the book of Isaiah are included in the hundreds of expressions employed by the Revelator in describing the enemies of Christ's church. In the Old Testament those passages were used to describe *national* Israel and the overthrow of their *national* enemies. When the Revelator makes use of these same texts he lifts them out of their literal and local setting, and gives them a *world-wide* and *anti-typical* meaning. The Revelator employs the Old Testament *pictures of the conflicts of national Israel and her enemies* to provide the *descriptive imagery* of the conflicts of the church of Jesus Christ with her foes.

THE DOOM OF BABYLON FORETOLD IN THE BOOK OF ISAIAH

The doom of literal Babylon is forecast in Isa., chapters, 13, 14. Isa. 14:12-14 sets forth Lucifer as the invisible Ruler of Babylon, which was overthrown because it had become the seat of Satan's worldly dominion. In describing the overthrow of spiritual Babylon, the Revelator employs imagery obtained from the prophetic pictures given in the Old Testament of the overthrow of ancient Babylon. The type and the anti-type must never be lost sight of in the study of the Revelation, or the meaning of the symbols will not be interpreted in their proper sense.

The Babylonians destroyed Jerusalem, burned down the magnificent Temple of Solomon which was the center of their religious and national life, and took the national people of God into captivity. Lucifer, the invisible king of spiritual Babylon, will unite his forces to attack and destroy the *church*—God's temple. 2 Cor. 6:16; Ephes. 2:20-22; Rev. 11:1, 2; etc.

Isaiah foretold the invasion of Palestine by the Babylonians to obtain possession of the wealth Hezekiah had shown them. Isa. 39:3-6. As usual, God did not leave His people to be fearful of the coming scourge. He immediately cheered them with words of "comfort." Isa. 40:1. He told them of His Almighty power. Isa. 40:12-26. By His wonderful providences He would cause the kings of the east to come against Babylon and destroy these oppressors of His people, and thus bring about their deliverance from the hands of the Babylonians. See Isa. 41:2, 25; 46:11. "The Lord hath raised up the spirit of the Kings of the Medes: for His device is against Babylon, to destroy it, because it is the vengeance of the Lord, the vengeance of His temple." Jer. 51:11. "Prepare against her the *nations* with the *kings* of the Medes, the captains thereof, and all the rulers thereof." Jer. 50:41, 42. See also Isa. 13:17; Dan. 8:20. Because Babylon was overthrown by *kings* from the east the Revelator, in describing the overthrow of spiritual Babylon, speaks of the coming of "the *kings* of the east." Rev. 16:12. In another *book* I have shown that "the kings of the east" can have reference only to *enemies of Babylon*. To apply these kings of the east, *in the description of the overthrow of Babylon*, to Japan or China reveals a failure to grasp the setting of the prophecy.

In bringing down ancient Babylon Cyrus dried up the waters of the Euphrates. See Isa. 44:27, 28; 45:1; Jer. 50:38; 51:32, 36. Hence the mention of the drying up of the waters of the Babylonian Euphrates in the Revelator's description of the overthrow of modern Babylon. Rev. 16:12; 17:1, 15. When Isaiah predicted the coming of the Babylonians God hastened to comfort His people by reminding them of His almighty power. Through the exercise of His power He would raise up Cyrus, the anointed—meaning the messiah—the type of Christ—who would lead other kings from the east, to destroy Israel's Babylonian oppressors.

It was at the commencement of the message of the coming deliverance from the hands of the Babylonians by Cyrus and the other kings of the east, that God declared: "I, the Lord, the first, and with the last; I am He." Isa. 41:4. This comforting truth is repeated in Isa. 43:10; 44:6; 48:12. These are the verses *Jesus quotes* in Revelation when referring to Himself as "the first and the last." In the book of Isaiah, the Son of God spoke of Himself as "the first and the last" when encouraging His people with the promise that He would overthrow their Babylonian enemies and bring them deliverance. In the Revelation, He again refers to Himself as "the first and the last" to encourage His *church* that He will overthrow the *anti-typical Babylon* and bring about their *eternal deliverance*.

As in Isaiah the Redeemer-King of Israel repeated this designation several times in outlining Babylon's doom, so in the Revelation, which gives an outline of the final doom of spiritual Babylon, He repeats several times that He is "the first and the last." The Apocalypse reveals to us the infinite superiority of Jesus, our Lord, over His enemies, who are couched under the symbolic term "Babylon." He is first on the field of battle—He is the "Almond" among the trees—He "hastens" (this is a play upon the meaning of the word "Almond"—see Jer. 1:11, 12) to perform His word in saving His people. And He will be the last on the field of conflict, for He will destroy His enemies and deliver His people. This is the message of the Book of Revelation.

As the Book of Isaiah repeats the statement that Israel's Redeemer-King is "the *first* and the last"—which statement is also repeated in the Apocalypse—and as the *first* and *last texts* in the *Epanados* employed in the first chapter of Revelation are quotations from the Book of *Isaiah,* we see the connection between Isaiah's description of the overthrow of *ancient* Babylon and John's prophecy of the destruction of *spiritual* Babylon. From the use of the number 8 in this Epanados we also learn that the number 8 is one of the keys to which God has directed us in order to thoroughly grasp all that is comprehended in the triumph of Jesus—Israel's Redeemer-King—over His Babylonian enemies.

As we have shown in another place, that triumph not only occurs at the second advent, but also after the millennium when, as clearly shown by definite texts of Scripture and also indicated by the use of the number eight, the whole of His enemies will be *literally* resurrected and, after a "little season" (Rev. 20:3, 7, 8), irretrievably destroyed in the greater, final triumph of the Lord.

The principle which enables us to interpret aright the last-day prophecies involving *spiritual Israel and her enemies* is clearly revealed in the Apocalypse.

All the proper names and designations of the Revelation are *spiritually* employed—except the New Jerusalem, which must be considered in relation to the millennium. Herein is revealed the divinely-appointed principle for the interpretation of the prophecies *concerning Israel*, namely, that the *spiritual* interpretation applies *until the second coming* of Christ. The millennium will divide the spiritual and the literal, just as the cross divided the literal economy of literal Israel and spiritual dispensation of spiritual Israel. See my *What is Armageddon?* pp. 62-80. For a fuller presentation of this principle, which is revealed in the analysis of such prophecies as the Revelation, Daniel, Matt. 24, Joel 3, Zech. 14, Ezek. 38, 39, etc., and also is *invariably adhered to in the Spirit of Prophecy*, see my *Armageddon—Before and After the Millennium,* which I hope to publish shortly.

The *spiritual* phase of Armageddon occurs before the millennium. That is, the *gathering* mentioned in Rev. 16:14-16 is a spiritual gathering, or, as *interpreted by the Spirit of Prophecy*, a unity of Satan-led forces in war against their Maker and His law. The *literal* phase of Armageddon occurs after the millennium. The gathering mentioned in Rev. 20:8, 9 will be a *literal gathering* of literal armies with *literal weapons* of war, marching against Christ and His church within the *literal New Jerusalem*. There is no necessity to depend *solely* upon the thoughts which are brought to view by the study of the number eight in the Apocalypse. They are given by the Holy Spirit as an interesting way of double-checking what He teaches us more plainly and simply in other ways. Mrs. E. G. White wrote concerning the Book of Revelation:—"This book demands *close*, prayerful study, lest it be interpreted according to the ideas of men.... In the Revelation the *deep things* of God are portrayed." Letter 16, January 27th, 1900.

According to the laws of repetition, of the first and the last, and of type and anti-type, the events connected with the downfall of *literal* Babylon are to be repeated on a world-wide scale. Hence the allusion in Rev. 16:12-16 to the overthrow of *spiritual* Babylon (v. 19) by the kings of the east. In Rev. 16:12, the waters of the Euphrates, undoubtedly, are the symbol of the people who add to Babylon's glory. Babylon "sitteth upon *many waters*." This statement in Rev. 17:1, which is a *quotation from Jer. 51:13*, is interpreted in Rev. 17:15: "*The waters*... where the whore sitteth are peoples, and *multitudes*, and nations, and tongues." The "multitudes," led by the teachings of the leaders of Babylon, will seek to destroy God's people, or, as in the figure of the flooding of the waters of the Euphrates, mentioned in Isa. 8:7, 8, the waters of Babylon will flood over the people of God. See *What is Armageddon?* pp. 50-53. Just immediately before the outpouring of the 6th plague the people doing the bidding of the Babylonian leaders will be on the point of destroying God's people. The crisis will come at the time of the 6th plague. See EW 283-285; GC 635-637. Then the 6th plague will be poured out upon the waters of the Babylonian Euphrates. The demonstrations of the mighty power of God on behalf of His people turn the hostile Babylonian "multitudes" from their murderous intentions, and they commence slaying each other. This welter of bloodshed is in progress when Jesus comes to complete the work of destroying the wicked.

At the second advent the "Leader and Commander" (the first text in the Epanados, quoted from Isa. 55:4) of the forces of righteousness will overthrow the forces of evil in the anti-typical conflict of Megiddo. Rev. 16:16. This final conflict is enlarged upon in Rev. 19:11-21. The "sharp sword" in Isaiah's prophecy (49:2), mentioned in the 8th quotation in the Epanados of Rev. 1:16, is here seen in action (Rev. 19:15) in the *anti-typical* "Armageddon," which results in the complete destruction of spiritual Babylon. There are many laws which govern the interpretation of the prophecies of the Bible, and by them we *know* that the conflict brought to view in Rev. 16:12-16 *cannot* refer to *nations fighting nations*. The *only* Scriptural application which can be made of the prophetic description of "Armageddon" is that it is an *anti-typical, world-wide* battle (partly based on the *"first" battle* fought at Megiddo (Judges 4 and 5), which was a battle between Israel and her devil-led foes)—a conflict between the forces of good and evil, in which Jesus, "the Leader and Commander" with the "sharp sword," will deliver His people from the hands of their Babylonian oppressors.

Christ rose on Sun-day (*Satan's* "Baal" or "Lord's" day) to demonstrate that He is Lord of all, and to prove that He is "the Invincible Son" of God. The first day of the week is mentioned 8 times in the New Testament because it is the *symbolic* number for His triumph over His foes—a triumph which brings everlasting life to His trusting children.

The number eight is employed in Scripture to point us to the resurrection when the new life will be given *physically* (or to the body) as it is now bestowed *spiritually* on accepting Jesus as Lord and Saviour. This is *symbolized* by the baptismal service when the *old* life is *symbolically buried* in the watery grave, and the believing soul rises to "walk in *newness* of *life*." The use of the number eight in the Epanados in the 1st chapter of Revelation shows that Jesus is the supreme Lord Who will destroy all His enemies. But their final and complete destruction will not be until the close of the 1,000 years of Rev. 20, or at the end of the seventh millennium, when the second phase—the *literal* phase—of Armageddon takes place. The *new* world is finally prepared as a home for the saints at the commencement of the eighth millennium. The resurrection of Christ, and *the baptism of each saint* points to the time when God "will make *all things new*." Rev. 21:5. The reader is directed to the same phraseology being used when applied to the *spiritual* life of the individual and to the *literal* new world. Compare Rev. 21:5 with the following: "If any man be in Christ, he is a *new* creature (Var. "More lit. there is a *new creation*"); old things are passed away; behold *all things* are become *new.*" 2 Cor. 5:17. Thus there must be a *spiritual* regeneration or new birth (John 3:3, 7; Titus 3:5) before the *literal* new birth or regeneration of the *physical* world. See Matt. 19:28; etc.

Similarly, the first phase of Armageddon before the millennium is a *spiritual gathering*—a *spiritual conflict*; the *literal gathering* to, and the *literal conflict* against Christ and His church within, the *literal New Jerusalem* occurs at the end of the millennium. The principle involved enables us not only to understand all the prophecies relating to Armageddon, but also makes clear to us the right application of so much of the Scriptures. By it, the Third Angel's Message as taught in the Spirit of Prophecy is proved beyond doubt to be the truth of God. "Thanks be to God, which giveth *us* the *victory* through our Lord Jesus Christ." 1 Cor. 15:57.

Publications by Louis F. Were
(available from LAYMEN MINISTRIES)

For a catalog of hundreds of Christian books, DVDs, CDs, study materials and more at discount prices, contact us:

LAYMEN MINISTRIES

414 Zapada Rd.
St. Maries, ID 83861
Orders: (800)245-1844   Office: (208)245-5388

Website/Bookstore: www.lmn.org